Ai Millionaire Mindset

20 Proven Strategies to Boost Profits and Efficiency

Augustus Blackmore

Contents

Ai Millionaire Mindset:
20 Proven Strategies to Boost Profits and Efficiency
by
AUGUSTUS BLACKMORE

Join my mailing list and receive a free eBook: Beginner's Guide to AI Investing: A simplified guide for investing in AI technologies or companies.
Visit my website: www.synapticstories.com

Your support as a reader is invaluable, especially as a small indie publisher. Knowing that my book may providing enjoyment in your life is incredibly fulfilling.

If you could spare a minute to leave your honest feedback on Amazon, it would be immensely helpful.

Your review not only aids in improving my future work but also guides other parents in their choice of educational resources.

Once again, thank you for being a part of this journey. Your thoughts and experiences with the book are truly appreciated!

To leave feedback
1. Open up your camera app.
2. Point your mobile device at the QR code below.
3. The review page will appear in your web browser.

Or visit Amazon search by
Ai Millionaire Mindset and Augustus Blackmore to the Amazon search

INTRODUCTION

Welcome to "AI Millionaire Mindset: 20 Proven Strategies to Boost Profits and Efficiency." In today's fast-paced business world, AI isn't just a buzzword—it's a game changer. Whether you're an entrepreneur looking to scale your startup or a business leader aiming to innovate, this course is your roadmap to leveraging AI for unprecedented growth.

Real Success Story: Pauline's Transformation

Let me tell you about Pauline, a friend and fellow entrepreneur who transformed her struggling startup into a market leader by embracing AI in just a few years. Here's how she did it:

- AI Chatbots for 24/7 Customer Support: Pauline integrated AI chatbots to provide round-the-clock assistance, enhancing customer satisfaction and freeing her team to focus on more complex tasks.
- Predictive Analytics for Market Trends: By utilizing predictive analytics, she could proactively anticipate market shifts and adjust her strategies.
- Automation of Routine Tasks: Automating repetitive processes allowed her team to channel their creativity and innovation into driving the business forward.

As a result, Pauline's company's efficiency soared, customer satisfaction improved, and profits skyrocketed. Her story is a testament to the transformative power of AI when combined with the right mindset.

Why This Course?

By enrolling in this course, you'll learn how to adopt a forward-thinking, innovation-driven mindset—the millionaire mindset—that sets you apart in the AI era. Here's what you can expect:

What You'll Gain:

1. Practical AI Strategies:

    - Automate Customer Interactions: Implement AI-driven chatbots and virtual assistants.
    - Harness Data Analytics: Use AI to make informed, data-driven decisions.

- AI-Driven Marketing Campaigns: Create personalized marketing strategies using machine learning.
- Enhance Supply Chain Management: Optimize logistics and inventory with AI tools.
- Improve Financial Forecasting: Utilize AI for accurate financial predictions.

2. Expert Insights:

   - Real-World Examples: Learn from successful businesses that have integrated AI.
   - Success Stories: Gain inspiration from entrepreneurs like Pauline, who have achieved remarkable growth through AI.

3. Competitive Edge:

   - Cutting-Edge Technologies: Stay ahead by adopting the latest AI advancements.
   - Innovative Tools: Access exclusive tools that give you a strategic advantage in your industry.

Join the AI Revolution

Pauline says, "Embracing AI didn't just improve my business; it transformed how we think and operate daily."

So, are you ready to revolutionize your business and embrace the future? Don't just witness the AI revolution—become a leader in it! Let's dive in and embark on your journey to becoming an AI-driven success story. The future is AI—don't get left behind.

Chapter 1: Embracing the AI Millionaire Mindset

The Transformative Power of AI in Business

In today's rapidly evolving business landscape, Artificial Intelligence (AI) is no longer a futuristic concept—it's a present reality reshaping industries across the globe. Imagine a world where mundane tasks are automated, data-driven insights guide your decisions, and personalized customer experiences set you apart from the competition. This is the power of AI—a tool that empowers businesses to innovate, grow, and thrive in an increasingly competitive market.

AI as a Competitive Necessity

Gone are the days when AI was accessible only to tech giants. Now, businesses of all sizes can harness its capabilities to streamline operations, enhance customer engagement, and unlock new revenue streams. Embracing AI isn't just an option; it's a strategic imperative for staying relevant and competitive.

To genuinely appreciate AI's impact, let's explore a real-life example of its transformative power.

Pauline's Success Story: Transforming a Small Business with AI

To illustrate the tangible impact of AI, let's delve into the inspiring journey of my college friend, Pauline.

From Hesitation to Innovation

Pauline runs a boutique flower bouquet preservation business. Initially, she hesitated to adopt new technologies, feeling overwhelmed by the complexity and unsure where to start. With a tech background or support network, she could expand her customer base and optimize her operations.

Discovering AI-Driven Marketing Analytics

Everything changed when Pauline discovered AI-powered marketing tools. She began using HubSpot, an inbound marketing and sales platform that leverages AI to analyze customer behavior, track preferences, and automate marketing campaigns.

- Identifying Customer Preferences: By analyzing data on customer interactions, Pauline noticed a growing interest in eco-friendly preservation methods.
- Tailoring Marketing Strategies: She used these insights to create targeted marketing campaigns, emphasizing her eco-friendly options.
- Automating Engagement: AI tools helped her send personalized emails and offers, nurturing leads more effectively.

Remarkable Results

Within six months, Pauline experienced:

- A 30% increase in sales.
- Higher customer engagement and satisfaction.
- Improved operational efficiency.

"Embracing AI transformed my business and how I connect with my customers," Pauline reflects. "It opened doors I didn't even know existed."

Pauline's success is just one example of how AI can revolutionize a business. Let's explore the multifaceted benefits AI offers.

The Multifaceted Benefits of AI

Building on Pauline's success, let's explore how AI can revolutionize various aspects of your business.

1. Automation of Repetitive Tasks

AI excels at handling routine tasks, freeing up your time to focus on strategic initiatives.

- Administrative Duties: Schedule management, invoicing, and data entry.
- Customer Interactions: Chatbots provide instant responses to common inquiries.
- Inventory Management: Automated tracking and reordering systems.

Example: An e-commerce store uses AI chatbots like Tidio or Chatfuel to handle customer service, reducing response times and increasing customer satisfaction.

2. Advanced Data Analysis

AI can quickly process vast amounts of data, uncovering insights that drive informed decisions.

- Customer Behavior: Analyze purchasing patterns to tailor marketing efforts.
- Market Trends: Predict shifts in the market to stay ahead of competitors.
- Operational Efficiency: Identify bottlenecks in your processes.

Example: A retailer uses AI analytics tools like Google Analytics or Tableau to determine peak shopping times and optimizes staff schedules and inventory levels accordingly.

3. Enhanced Decision-Making with Predictive Analytics

AI's predictive capabilities help forecast future trends based on historical data.

- Sales Forecasting: Anticipate demand to manage supply chains effectively.
- Risk Assessment: Evaluate potential risks in investment opportunities.
- Personalized Recommendations: Offer customers products they're likely to buy.

Example: Streaming services like Netflix and Spotify use AI algorithms to recommend content based on user history, increasing engagement.

While these benefits are significant, AI's impact extends across various industries, driving innovation and growth on a global scale.

AI as a Catalyst for Innovation Across Industries

AI's impact isn't limited to a single sector. Let's examine how various industries leverage AI for groundbreaking advancements.

Healthcare

- Diagnostics: AI algorithms analyze medical images and patient data for early disease detection.
- Personalized Treatment: Tailor treatments based on genetic information.
- Operational Efficiency: Optimize staff scheduling and resource allocation.

Case Study: Hospitals using AI-powered diagnostic tools like IBM Watson Health have reduced misdiagnosis rates by up to 15%, improving patient outcomes.

Finance

- Real-Time Analytics: Monitor financial markets and execute trades at optimal times.
- Fraud Detection: Identify unusual transactions to prevent fraud.
- Customer Service: Chatbots assist customers with account inquiries and transac-

tions.

Case Study: Banks implementing AI for fraud detection, such as HSBC with their AI system Quantexa, have seen a 20% decrease in fraudulent activities.

Cybersecurity

- Threat Detection: AI identifies and neutralizes cyber threats in real-time.
- Vulnerability Assessment: Continuously scans systems for weaknesses.
- Incident Response: Automates responses to security breaches.

Case Study: Companies using AI-driven cybersecurity solutions like Darktrace have reduced incident response times by 60%.

Agriculture

- Crop Monitoring: AI drones assess crop health and optimize irrigation.
- Yield Prediction: Predict harvest volumes to plan logistics.
- Pest Detection: Early identification of pest infestations.

Example: Farms using AI platforms like Prospera have increased yields by optimizing resource usage.

As we see, AI's potential is vast, but adopting it requires not just technological changes but also a shift in mindset.

Developing a Millionaire Mindset with AI Technology

Adopting AI is as much a mindset shift as a technological upgrade. Here's how to cultivate the AI Millionaire Mindset:

1. Embrace Continuous Learning
   - Stay Informed: Keep up with AI trends and advancements.
   - Invest in Education: Attend workshops, webinars, and courses on AI applications.
   - Foster a Learning Culture: Encourage your team to develop AI-related skills.

Action Step: Subscribe to industry journals like MIT Technology Review or join professional networks like AI Business.

2. Seek Personalized Advice and Mentorship
   - Consult Experts: Engage with AI consultants to identify opportunities.
   - Join Communities: Participate in forums like Reddit's r/artificial or LinkedIn groups where you can share experiences.

- Mentorship Programs: Find mentors who have successfully integrated AI into their businesses.

Reflection Prompt: Who can you connect with to gain insights into effectively leveraging AI? Consider reaching out to industry leaders or joining a mentorship program.

3. Take Strategic Action with an Open Mind
    - Pilot Programs: Start small with AI initiatives to test their impact.
    - Be Adaptable: Remain open to changing strategies based on AI insights.
    - Measure Impact: Use Key Performance Indicators (KPIs) to assess the effectiveness of AI implementations.

Example: Implement an AI chatbot on your website using platforms like ManyChat or MobileMonkey and monitor its effect on customer engagement over three months.

While embracing AI offers numerous benefits, it's essential to be aware of potential challenges and ethical considerations.

Overcoming Challenges and Ethical Considerations in Adopting AI

Transitioning to AI-driven operations may present challenges and ethical implications.

1. Understanding Big Data
    - Challenge: Interpreting large datasets can be overwhelming.
    - Solution: Use AI analytics tools like Microsoft Power BI or Looker to visualize data and highlight key insights.
2. Resource Constraints
    - Challenge: Limited budget or technical expertise.
    - Solution: Start with cost-effective AI solutions like Zoho CRM for automation or Hootsuite for social media management, and consider cloud-based services that require less infrastructure.
3. Resistance to Change
    - Challenge: Team members may be hesitant to adopt new technologies.
    - Solution: Communicate the benefits clearly and provide training to ease the transition.

Action Step: Identify potential barriers in your organization and develop a plan to address them, including training programs and open discussions.

4. Ethical Considerations
    - Data Privacy: Ensure compliance with regulations like GDPR and protect customer

data.

- Job Displacement: Be mindful of how automation may affect employment and consider retraining opportunities for staff.
- Bias in AI: Monitor AI systems for unintended biases to promote fairness.

Best Practice: Adopt responsible AI policies and involve stakeholders in discussions about ethical use. Understanding and addressing these challenges will position your business to harness AI effectively and responsibly.

Grasping the Bigger Picture

To fully embrace the AI millionaire mindset, it's essential to understand the broader implications of AI integration:

- Global Competitiveness: AI adoption positions your business on the cutting edge, ready to compete globally.
- Customer Expectations: Modern customers expect personalized, efficient experiences that AI can deliver.
- Sustainability and Scalability: AI solutions often lead to more sustainable practices and can scale with your business growth.

Case Study: According to a study by Accenture, companies that have integrated AI into their core operations report growth rates up to 50% faster than those that haven't.

Now that we've explored the potential of AI and how to approach it, let's consider practical steps you can take to start implementing AI in your business.

Harnessing the Power of AI: Next Steps

Reflect on areas within your business where AI could make a significant impact.

1. Automating Routine Tasks

Opportunity: Free up time and resources by automating administrative duties.

Action Step: Identify time-consuming but low-complexity tasks. Consider using tools like Zapier for workflow automation or Xero for accounting.

2. Enhancing Customer Engagement

Opportunity: Use AI to provide personalized customer interactions.

Action Step: Implement chatbots or AI-driven email marketing campaigns using platforms like Mailchimp with AI features.

3. Deepening Data Insights

Opportunity: Leverage AI analytics to make data-driven decisions.

Action Step: Adopt AI tools, such as Salesforce Einstein Analytics, that analyze sales data, customer behavior, or market trends.

Reflection Prompt: Choose one area to focus on initially. What steps can you take this week to explore AI solutions in that domain? Perhaps schedule a demo, sign up for a trial, or consult with a vendor.

These steps will set you on the path to effectively integrating AI into your business.

Conclusion: Embrace the Future with Confidence

The future belongs to those who embrace innovation and are willing to adapt to new technologies. By integrating AI into your business strategy, you're not just keeping up with the times—you're setting the stage for exponential growth and success.

Key Takeaways:

- AI is Accessible: Tools and platforms are available for businesses of all sizes.
- Mindset Matters: Cultivating an open, growth-oriented mindset is crucial.
- Action is Essential: Start small, but start now. Even minor AI implementations can have significant impacts.
- Responsible Adoption: Be mindful of ethical considerations to ensure sustainable success.

Take the first step toward becoming an AI-driven success story. Explore AI tools relevant to your industry, connect with experts, and begin your journey toward the AI millionaire mindset.

In the next chapter, we'll delve deeper into specific AI tools and strategies you can implement to transform your business operations and achieve your goals.

Chapter 2: Harnessing the Power of ChatGPT

Introduction: Unleashing the Future with ChatGPT

Imagine having a personal assistant who can draft emails, write code, generate creative content, and answer complex questions—all within seconds. Welcome to the world of ChatGPT, a revolutionary AI language model that's transforming how we work, learn, and communicate. In this chapter, we'll explore how ChatGPT is reshaping industries, enhancing productivity, and opening up new possibilities for innovation. You'll discover practical ways to leverage ChatGPT in your personal and professional life, understand its capabilities and limitations, and learn how to maximize its potential responsibly.

Understanding ChatGPT

What Is ChatGPT?

ChatGPT is a powerful Large Language Model (LLM) developed by OpenAI. Trained on vast amounts of text data, it can generate coherent and contextually relevant responses based on the prompts it receives. Think of it as a highly knowledgeable virtual assistant available 24/7, ready to assist with tasks ranging from drafting emails to providing coding support.

Note: While ChatGPT is an impressive tool, it's important to remember that it may occasionally produce inaccurate information or need more awareness of events after its last update (as of September 2021). Always verify critical facts with reliable sources.

Key Capabilities of ChatGPT

1. Generating Human-Like Responses

One of ChatGPT's most remarkable features is its ability to produce text that closely resembles human writing. It's adept at understanding context and can mimic various tones and styles, making it invaluable for crafting personalized messages.

Example:

Need to write a professional apology email to a client regarding a delayed project? You might prompt:

"Compose a sincere apology email to a client explaining a two-week delay in their project delivery due to unforeseen circumstances."

2. Educational Assistance

ChatGPT is an effective educational tool that aids students and lifelong learners in understanding complex concepts, preparing for exams, and generate study materials.

Example:

A student struggling with chemistry might ask:

"Explain the concept of chemical equilibrium in simple terms suitable for a high school student."

ChatGPT Response:

Chemical equilibrium occurs when a chemical reaction and its reverse reaction happen at the same rate. This means that the concentrations of reactants and products remain constant over time. Imagine you're filling a bathtub with water while the drain is open. Eventually, the water level stops rising because the rate at which water flows in equals the rate at which it flows out. Similarly, in chemical equilibrium, the forward and reverse reactions balance each other, keeping the system stable.

Reflection Prompt: If you had access to ChatGPT during your education, which subjects would you find most helpful?

3. Content Creation

ChatGPT can be a game-changer for writers, marketers, and content creators. It assists in generating ideas, creating outlines, and even drafting entire articles or social media posts.

Example:

A blogger experiencing writer's block could prompt:

"Outline a blog post on the top five benefits of a plant-based diet."

ChatGPT Response:

Outline: Top Five Benefits of Adopting a Plant-Based Diet

1. Improved Health
    - Lower risk of chronic diseases
    - Better weight management
2. Environmental Sustainability
    - Reduced carbon footprint
    - Conservation of water resources
3. Animal Welfare
    - Ethical treatment of animals

- Decreased demand for factory farming

4. Economic Savings
    - Lower grocery bills
    - Reduced healthcare costs
5. Enhanced Energy Levels
    - Increased nutrient intake
    - Improved digestion

Reflection Prompt: Think about when starting a writing project was challenging. How might ChatGPT have helped you overcome that hurdle?

4. Coding Support

Developers can leverage ChatGPT for generating code snippets, debugging assistance, and learning new programming languages.

Example:

If you're interested in creating a simple web page, you might ask:

"Provide HTML and CSS code for a basic personal portfolio webpage."

Reflection Prompt: What coding projects have you wanted to tackle, and how could ChatGPT assist you in starting them?

Real-World Applications and Success Stories

Business Enhancement

Businesses across industries are integrating ChatGPT to improve efficiency, customer engagement, and innovation.

Customer Support Automation: A tech startup utilized ChatGPT to handle common customer inquiries, reducing response times by 60% and significantly boosting customer satisfaction. Their support team could focus on more complex issues by automating routine queries improving overall service quality.

Marketing Content Generation: A freelance marketer increased productivity by 50% by using ChatGPT to draft social media posts and marketing emails, enabling more time for strategy development.

Case Study: Samantha runs a social media agency and often faces tight deadlines. Using ChatGPT to generate initial drafts of posts, she meets deadlines more comfortably and focuses on client relations.

Educational Impact

Educators and students use ChatGPT to enhance learning experiences.

Lesson Planning: Teachers generate interactive lesson plans and quiz questions, saving preparation time.

Example: A teacher might prompt:

"Create a quiz with ten multiple-choice questions on the causes of World War II for high school students."

Study Assistance: Students receive explanations of complex topics, aiding in comprehension and retention.

Example: A university student uses ChatGPT to study for finals by inputting:

"Summarize the key themes of Shakespeare's 'Hamlet' in simple terms."

Healthcare Innovations

In healthcare, professionals leverage ChatGPT to streamline administrative tasks and improve patient communication.

Patient Education Materials: Medical staff use ChatGPT to draft understandable explanations of medical procedures or conditions for patients.

Example: A doctor might prompt:

"Explain the process of an MRI scan in simple terms for a patient brochure."

Financial Services

Financial institutions utilize ChatGPT to draft reports, analyze market trends, and enhance customer service.

Market Analysis Summaries: Analysts use ChatGPT to condense complex financial data into digestible summaries.

Example: An analyst might ask:

"Summarize the recent trends in cryptocurrency markets for a client newsletter."

Limitations and Ethical Considerations

Accuracy and Reliability

Knowledge Cutoff: ChatGPT's training data includes information up to its last update (September 2021). It may need to be made aware of recent developments.

Misinformation Risk: Occasionally, ChatGPT may produce incorrect or misleading information.

Action Point: Verify important information through reputable sources to ensure accuracy.

AI Bias and Fairness

Potential Biases: ChatGPT may reflect biases in its training data, leading to unintentional prejudice in responses.

Best Practice: Be mindful of potential biases and critically evaluate AI-generated content, especially concerning sensitive topics.

Data Privacy Concerns

Confidentiality: Avoid sharing sensitive personal or business information in your prompts, as the data entered could be stored or used to improve the model.

Best Practice: Use generalized or anonymized data when necessary, and refrain from inputting proprietary information.

Ethical Use in Academia and Business

Academic Integrity: Using ChatGPT to complete assignments without proper attribution constitutes plagiarism.

Responsible Utilization: Incorporate your insights and expertise using ChatGPT to enhance, not replace, your work.

Maximizing ChatGPT's Potential

Effective Prompting

Be Specific and Clear: Detailed prompts yield more accurate and valuable responses.

Example: Instead of asking, "Tell me about marketing," you could ask, "Explain the key differences between digital marketing and traditional marketing."

Iterative Interaction: Engage in a dialogue with ChatGPT by asking follow-up questions or requesting revisions.

Example:

- Initial Prompt: "Draft an introduction for a report on sustainable business practices."
- Follow-up Prompt: "Now, include recent examples of companies successfully im-

plementing these practices."

Actionable Exercise: Try crafting a prompt for a task you need assistance with. Analyze the response and consider how it can be improved—experiment with rephrasing or adding details to your prompt.

Combining AI with Human Expertise

Augmentation, Not Replacement: Use ChatGPT to support your skills, not replace them.

Critical Evaluation: Assess the AI's output critically and adjust as needed.

Reflection Prompt: How can you integrate ChatGPT's suggestions with your expertise to produce optimal results?

Managing Unsatisfactory Responses

Refining Prompts: If the output isn't helpful, rephrase your prompt or provide more context.

Understanding Limitations: Recognize that ChatGPT may only sometimes grasp nuances with sufficient background information.

Best Practice: Continuously refine your prompts and provide detailed context to improve the quality of responses.

Real-World Applications and Success Stories (Expanded)

Agriculture

Crop Monitoring: AI drones assess crop health and optimize irrigation.

Yield Prediction: Predict harvest volumes to plan logistics.

Pest Detection: Early identification of pest infestations.

Example: Farms using AI platforms like Prospera have increased yields by optimizing resource usage, resulting in a 15% boost in productivity.

Future Developments

ChatGPT is expected to gain new features and improvements as AI technology evolves.

Latest Features and Anticipated Updates

Multimodal Inputs: Future versions may handle visual inputs, such as images or graphs, expanding possibilities for data analysis and creative projects.

Plugin Integrations: The introduction of plugins allows ChatGPT to access up-to-date information and perform tasks like booking appointments or retrieving real-time data.

Enhanced Context Understanding: Ongoing updates aim to improve ChatGPT's ability to maintain context over extended conversations, making interactions more coherent.

Stay Informed: Stay updated with the latest developments to leverage new capabilities effectively. Visit OpenAI's website for updates and resources.

Additional Resources

- OpenAI's Official Guidelines: Learn more about effective prompting and best practices at OpenAI's Help Center.

- Community Forums: Engage with other users to share experiences and tips on platforms like Reddit's r/OpenAI.

- Educational Materials: Explore online courses on AI and ChatGPT from platforms like Coursera, Udemy, and edX.

- Tools and Software Recommendations: Utilize platforms like Zapier for workflow automation, Tidio for chatbots, and Tableau for data visualization.

Embracing ChatGPT's Power

ChatGPT is revolutionizing how we approach communication, education, and business operations. By understanding its strengths and limitations, you can harness this tool to enhance productivity, stimulate creativity, and drive innovation in your endeavors.

Key Takeaways:

- Versatility Across Fields: ChatGPT offers applications in content creation, coding support, customer service, and more.

- Effective Use Requires Strategy: Clear prompting, critical evaluation, and ethical considerations are essential for maximizing benefits.

- Stay Updated: Keeping informed about the latest features ensures you leverage ChatGPT's full potential.

Action Step: Identify a task for which ChatGPT could assist you today. Whether drafting an email, creating an outline, or generating code, experiment with specific prompts and observe how ChatGPT can transform your workflow.

Engagement Exercise

Action Item: Choose a project or task you're currently working on. Use ChatGPT to assist with a component, such as drafting an email, creating an outline, or generating code.

Reflect: Assess the quality of the AI's output. What worked well? What needed adjustment? How did it enhance your productivity?

Example: If you're preparing a presentation, ask ChatGPT to draft the introduction or summarize key points. Evaluate how these drafts fit into your presentation and refine them as needed.

Conclusion: Embrace the Future with Confidence

The future belongs to those who embrace innovation and are willing to adapt to new technologies. By integrating AI into your business strategy, you're not just keeping up with the times—you're setting the stage for exponential growth and success.

Key Takeaways:

- AI is Accessible: Tools and platforms are available for businesses of all sizes.
- Mindset Matters: Cultivating an open, growth-oriented mindset is crucial.
- Action is Essential: Start small, but start now. Even minor AI implementations can have significant impacts.
- Responsible Adoption: Be mindful of ethical considerations to ensure sustainable success.

Take the first step toward becoming an AI-driven success story. Explore AI tools relevant to your industry, connect with experts, and begin your journey toward the AI millionaire mindset.

In the next chapter, we'll delve deeper into specific AI tools and strategies you can implement to transform your business operations and achieve your goals.

Chapter 3: Strategy 1 – AI-Driven Content Creation

Introduction: AI is the Backbone of Modern Content Creation

In the digital age, content is king. High-quality content attracts audiences, builds brand reputation, and drives business growth. However, consistently creating compelling content can be challenging. What if you could harness the power of Artificial Intelligence (AI) to streamline this process? Enter ChatGPT, a revolutionary tool that transforms content creation by making it more efficient, creative, and scalable.

1. Brainstorming Topic Ideas

Generating fresh and relevant topics is the first step in content creation. ChatGPT can help you brainstorm ideas tailored to your audience's interests, ensuring your content remains engaging and pertinent.

Example:

- Prompt: "Generate ten blog post ideas about eco-friendly living for a sustainability blog."

Tip: Customize the prompts to reflect your unique voice and niche to ensure the ideas align with your brand and audience preferences.

Action Step: Use ChatGPT to generate a list of potential topics for your next content cycle. Review and select the most relevant ones to maintain consistency and engagement.

Reflection Prompt: How can diversifying your content topics improve audience engagement and retention?

2. Performing Keyword Research

Effective keyword research enhances your content's visibility by aligning it with what your audience is searching for. ChatGPT can assist in identifying relevant keywords that drive traffic and improve SEO.

Example:

- Prompt: "List long-tail keywords related to 'digital marketing trends in 2024.'"

Stat Insight: According to a SEMrush study, 68% of marketers consider keyword research crucial for their SEO strategy.

Tip: Combine AI-generated keywords with tools like Ahrefs, SEMrush, or Google Keyword Planner for comprehensive analysis and validation.

Action Step: To boost SEO performance, naturally incorporate identified keywords into your content, including titles, headers, and meta descriptions.

Reflection Prompt: How can integrating long-tail keywords improve your content's search engine ranking and attract a more targeted audience?

Advanced SEO Techniques

To further enhance your SEO strategy, consider implementing advanced techniques that go beyond essential keyword integration:

1. Semantic SEO:
   - Description: Focus on the intent behind the keywords and incorporate related terms and concepts to provide comprehensive coverage of the topic.
   - Implementation: Use ChatGPT to generate semantically related terms and integrate them naturally into your content.
   - Example Prompt: "List semantically related terms for 'sustainable fashion trends 2024.'"
2. LSI (Latent Semantic Indexing) Keywords:
   - Description: These keywords are conceptually related to your primary keywords, helping search engines understand the context of your content.
   - Implementation: Use AI to identify LSI keywords and include them to enhance content relevance.
   - Example Prompt: "Provide LSI keywords for 'remote work productivity tips.'"
3. Structured Data and Schema Markup:
   - Description: Implementing structured data helps search engines better understand your content, potentially leading to rich snippets in search results.
   - Implementation: Use AI to generate schema markup for different types of content.
   - Example Prompt: "Create schema markup for a blog post about 'AI in Healthc are.'"

4. Content Clusters and Pillar Pages:

   ◦ Description: Organize content into clusters around a central pillar page to improve site architecture and SEO.

   ◦ Implementation: Use ChatGPT to outline content clusters and related subtopics.

   ◦ Example Prompt: "Outline a content cluster around the pillar topic 'Digital Marketing Strategies.'"

Case Study: Advanced SEO Implementation by GreenTech Blog GreenTech Blog aimed to improve its SEO performance by implementing semantic SEO and structured data. Using ChatGPT, they identified semantically related terms and LSI keywords for their articles on renewable energy. Additionally, they integrated schema markup to enhance search engine understanding. As a result, their organic traffic increased by 40% within six months, and their articles began appearing in rich snippets.

3. Conducting Competitor Analysis

Understanding your competitors helps you identify content gaps and opportunities to differentiate your offerings. ChatGPT can streamline competitor analysis by highlighting areas where competitors excel or fall short.

Steps:

1. Identify Competitors: Use tools like Ahrefs, SEMrush, or Moz to list your top competitors.

2. Analyze Content: Examine their content's topics, keywords, and engagement levels.

3. Find Gaps: Identify areas they still need to cover in-depth, providing opportunities for your unique content.

Example:

- Prompt: "What topics related to 'remote work challenges' are underrepresented by top industry blogs?"

Case Study: Tech Innovators Inc. conducted a competitor analysis using ChatGPT and discovered a lack of content on mental health strategies for remote workers. They created a comprehensive guide on this topic, resulting in a 25% increase in website traffic and higher engagement rates.

Tip: Regularly perform competitor analyses to stay ahead of industry trends and continuously refine your content strategy.

Action Step: Use ChatGPT to generate a list of potential content gaps based on competitor analysis and prioritize them for your content calendar.

Reflection Prompt: What unique perspectives can you bring to underrepresented topics in your industry to attract and engage your audience?

4. Generating Outlines and Long-Form Content

With topics and keywords ready, creating detailed outlines helps organize your content logically and coherently. ChatGPT can assist in structuring your articles, ensuring comprehensive coverage of each subject.

Example:

- Prompt: "Create an outline for an article titled 'The Impact of AI on Healthcare in 2024.'"

Tip: Personalize and expand the outline with your insights and expertise to add unique value and depth to your content.

Action Step: Develop each outline section, ensuring comprehensive coverage and seamless flow between topics.

Reflection Prompt: How can a well-structured outline improve the quality and coherence of your long-form content?

5. Researching Content

While ChatGPT provides valuable information, verifying facts with up-to-date and reliable sources is essential to maintain content accuracy and credibility.

Best Practices:

- Cross-Reference Data: Use reputable publications, studies, or official reports to validate information provided by ChatGPT.

- Update Statistics: Ensure all data is current, especially in rapidly evolving AI and digital marketing fields.

Example:

- Prompt: "Provide recent statistics on the effectiveness of AI in content marketing."

Tip: Include links to sources or citations within your content to enhance credibility.

Action Step: After generating content with ChatGPT, create a checklist to verify all facts and update outdated information.

Reflection Prompt: How does ensuring content accuracy influence your audience's trust and your brand's reputation?

6. Adding an FAQ Section

An FAQ section addresses common queries, enhancing user engagement and improving SEO by incorporating relevant keywords naturally.

Example:

- Prompt: "Generate five FAQs about 'electric vehicles in urban areas' with concise answers."

Tip: Use AI-generated FAQs to anticipate and address your audience's most pressing questions, enhancing user satisfaction and SEO performance.

Action Step: Incorporate an FAQ section at the end of your articles or web pages to provide quick answers and improve search engine rankings.

Reflection Prompt: How can an effective FAQ section enhance your content's value and user experience?

7. Ensuring On-Page SEO Optimization

Optimizing content for search engines ensures higher visibility and better ranking, driving more organic traffic to your site. ChatGPT can assist in seamlessly incorporating SEO best practices.

Steps:

1. Meta Titles and Descriptions: Use ChatGPT to craft compelling meta titles and descriptions with targeted keywords.
    - Example:
        - Prompt: "Write a meta description for an article on 'Healthy Eating Habits for Busy Professionals.'"
        - ChatGPT Response: "Discover practical tips to maintain healthy eating despite a hectic schedule. Boost your energy and productivity with simple dietary changes."
2. Header Tags: Organize content with H1, H2, and H3 tags to improve readability and SEO.
    - H1: Main title of the article.
    - H2: Subheadings for primary sections.
    - H3: Sub-subheadings for detailed points.
3. Alt Text for Images: Describe images accurately to improve accessibility and SEO.
    - Example:

- Prompt: "Write an alt text for an image showing a person working on a laptop in a coffee shop."
- ChatGPT Response: "Person working on a laptop in a cozy coffee shop, illustrating remote work flexibility."

Tip: Incorporate keywords naturally within the content to avoid keyword stuffing and maintain readability and engagement.

Action Step: Utilize ChatGPT to generate SEO-friendly meta tags and alt texts, ensuring they align with your overall SEO strategy.

Reflection Prompt: How does effective on-page SEO optimization influence your content's search engine ranking and visibility?

Advanced SEO Techniques

To further enhance your SEO strategy, consider implementing advanced techniques that go beyond essential keyword integration:

1. Semantic SEO:
    - Description: Focus on the intent behind the keywords and incorporate related terms and concepts to provide comprehensive coverage of the topic.
    - Implementation: Use ChatGPT to generate semantically related terms and integrate them naturally into your content.
    - Example Prompt: "List semantically related terms for 'sustainable fashion trends 2024.'"
2. LSI (Latent Semantic Indexing) Keywords:
    - Description: These keywords are conceptually related to your primary keywords, helping search engines understand the context of your content.
    - Implementation: Use AI to identify LSI keywords and include them to enhance content relevance.
    - Example Prompt: "Provide LSI keywords for 'remote work productivity tips.'"
3. Structured Data and Schema Markup:
    - Description: Implementing structured data helps search engines better understand your content, potentially leading to rich snippets in search results.
    - Implementation: Use AI to generate schema markup for different types of content.

- Example Prompt: "Create schema markup for a blog post about 'AI in Healthcare.'"

4. Content Clusters and Pillar Pages:

   - Description: Organize content into clusters around a central pillar page to improve site architecture and SEO.
   - Implementation: Use ChatGPT to outline content clusters and related subtopics.
   - Example Prompt: "Outline a content cluster around the pillar topic 'Digital Marketing Strategies.'"

Case Study: Advanced SEO Implementation by GreenTech Blog GreenTech Blog aimed to improve its SEO performance by implementing semantic SEO and structured data. Using ChatGPT, they identified semantically related terms and LSI keywords for their articles on renewable energy. Additionally, they integrated schema markup to enhance search engine understanding. As a result, their organic traffic increased by 40% within six months, and their articles began appearing in rich snippets.

8. Monetizing AI-Generated Content

Monetization strategies transform your content into revenue-generating assets. ChatGPT can assist in identifying and effectively implementing various monetization methods.

Monetization Strategies:

1. Affiliate Marketing:

   - Description: Promote products related to your content and earn commissions on sales through referral links.
   - Example: Write a blog post on eco-friendly products, including affiliate links to sustainable brands.

2. Sponsored Posts:

   - Description: Collaborate with brands to create content that promotes their products or services.
   - Example: Partnering with a tech company to write a review of their latest gadget.

3. Ad Revenue:

- Description: Utilize platforms like Google AdSense to display ads on your website, earning revenue based on impressions and clicks.
- Example: Placing banner ads on high-traffic blog pages to generate passive income.

Ethical Considerations:

1. Transparency:
   - Description: Disclose sponsored content and affiliate relationships to maintain trust with your audience.
   - Example: Including disclaimers like "This post contains affiliate links. I may earn a commission if you purchase through these links."
2. Value Addition:
   - Description: Ensure monetized content provides genuine value and benefits to your readers.
   - Example: Writing honest reviews and recommendations based on personal experiences with products.

Tip: Balance monetization efforts with quality content to avoid compromising your audience's trust and engagement.

Action Step: Identify suitable monetization strategies for your content niche and implement them thoughtfully, ensuring they align with your brand values and audience interests.

Reflection Prompt: How can you integrate monetization strategies without detracting from the quality and integrity of your content?

9. Ethics and Quality in AI-Generated Content

Maintaining integrity and quality is paramount when using AI for content creation. Adhering to ethical guidelines ensures your content remains trustworthy and valuable.

Guidelines:

1. Transparency:
   - Description: Inform readers if the content is AI-assisted when appropriate to maintain honesty and trust.
   - Example: Adding a note like "This article was created with AI tools to enhance content quality."
2. Fact-Checking:

- Description: Verify that all information provided by ChatGPT is from reliable sources to prevent the dissemination of misinformation.
- Example: Cross-referencing statistics and claims with authoritative studies or official reports.

3. Originality:
    - Description: Add your unique perspective and insights to AI-generated content to differentiate it and provide added value.
    - Example: Incorporating personal experiences or expert opinions to enrich the content.
4. Bias Awareness:
    - Description: Review content for potential biases or inaccuracies to ensure fairness and accuracy.
    - Example: Assessing AI-generated responses for unintentional prejudice, especially in sensitive topics, and making necessary adjustments.

Best Practices:

1. Maintain a Human Touch: Use AI as a supportive tool, combining it with your creativity and expertise to produce high-quality content.
2. Regular Audits: Review AI-generated content for compliance with ethical standards and quality benchmarks.
3. Continuous Improvement: Update and refine AI prompts and guidelines based on feedback and evolving best practices.

Establish a content review process with AI assistance and human oversight to ensure consistency and quality.

Action Step: Develop a checklist for reviewing AI-generated content, emphasizing transparency, accuracy, originality, and bias mitigation.

Reflection Prompt: How can ethical guidelines in AI-generated content enhance your credibility and audience trust?

10. Common Challenges and Solutions in AI-Driven Content Creation

While AI tools like ChatGPT offer numerous advantages in content creation, they also come with challenges. Proactively addressing these challenges ensures you can harness AI effectively without compromising quality or integrity.

Common Challenges:

1. Maintaining Originality and Avoiding Plagiarism:
    - Challenge: AI-generated content may inadvertently mimic existing content, leading to potential plagiarism issues.
    - Solution: Always review and edit AI-generated content to infuse your unique voice and ensure originality. Use plagiarism detection tools like Grammarly or Copyscape to verify content uniqueness.
2. Ensuring Content Accuracy:
    - Challenge: AI may produce information that needs to be updated or corrected.
    - Solution: Implement a rigorous fact-checking process. Cross-reference AI outputs with reliable sources and update data regularly to maintain accuracy.
3. Balancing AI Assistance with Human Creativity:
    - Challenge: Over-reliance on AI can result in generic or less engaging content.
    - Solution: Use AI as a starting point for ideas and drafts, then refine and enhance the content with your creativity and insights to make it more engaging and personalized.
4. Managing SEO and Readability:
    - Challenge: AI might prioritize SEO over readability, leading to search-engine-optimized content that is difficult for readers to engage with.
    - Solution: Balance SEO best practices with natural language and readability. Use AI to assist with SEO elements, but ensure the final content is reader-friendly by editing for flow and clarity.
5. Handling Sensitive Topics:
    - Challenge: AI may generate inappropriate or insensitive content and susceptible subjects.
    - Solution: Carefully review AI-generated content on sensitive topics. Implement guidelines and ethical standards to ensure respectful and accurate representation.
6. Integration with Existing Workflows:
    - Challenge: Incorporating AI tools into established content creation workflows

can be disruptive.

- Solution: Gradually integrate AI tools by starting with specific tasks (e.g., brainstorming or keyword research) and expanding their use as you become more comfortable. Provide training and resources to your team to facilitate smooth adoption.

Best Practices to Overcome Challenges:

1. Establish Clear Guidelines: Define how and when to use AI to maintain consistency and quality in your content creation process.

2. Continuous Training: Stay updated with the latest AI developments and train your team to use AI tools effectively.

3. Feedback Loops: Create mechanisms for regular feedback on AI-generated content to identify areas for improvement and adjust strategies accordingly.

4. Human Oversight: Ensure that all AI-generated content undergoes human review to maintain standards and address any issues promptly.

Case Study: Overcoming AI Challenges at HealthPlus Blog HealthPlus Blog integrated ChatGPT into their content creation process to streamline article drafting. Initially, they faced issues with maintaining originality and ensuring content accuracy. They enhanced content uniqueness and reliability by implementing a strict review process and using plagiarism detection tools. Additionally, they trained their writers to refine AI drafts with personal insights, resulting in more engaging and trustworthy articles. This balanced approach led to a 30% increase in reader engagement and a significant boost in search engine rankings.

Action Step: Identify the challenges in your content creation process and develop strategies using AI tools to address them effectively.

Reflection Prompt: What potential challenges might you encounter when integrating AI into your content creation, and how can you proactively address them to ensure success?

Conclusion: Elevate Your Content Creation with AI

AI-driven tools like ChatGPT can revolutionize your content creation process, enhancing efficiency and creativity. Integrating AI thoughtfully ensures high-quality standards while benefiting from increased productivity and innovation. Embrace AI as a powerful ally in your content strategy, and leverage its capabilities to stay ahead in the competitive digital landscape.

Key Takeaways:

- AI is a Tool, Not a Replacement: Combine AI capabilities with human creativity to produce compelling and authentic content.

- Quality Over Quantity: Focus on creating valuable and engaging content that resonates with your audience.
- Ethics Matter: Uphold transparency, integrity, and fairness in all AI-assisted content creation endeavors.
- Strategic Monetization: Implement monetization strategies that align with your brand and provide genuine value to your audience.

Action Steps:

1. Implement AI Tools: To streamline your workflow, start using ChatGPT for brainstorming, keyword research, and content drafting.
2. Optimize for SEO: Utilize AI to enhance your on-page SEO, ensuring your content reaches a broader audience.
3. Monetize Thoughtfully: Explore and integrate monetization strategies that align with your content and audience needs.
4. Maintain Ethical Standards: Establish guidelines to ensure your AI-generated content remains accurate, original, and unbiased.
5. Continuous Learning: Stay updated with AI advancements and refine your content creation strategies.

Reflection Prompt:

Consider a recent content project you worked on. How could AI have improved your process? Reflect on balancing AI assistance and your creative input to enhance efficiency and quality.

Additional Resources:

- SEO Tools: Ahrefs, SEMrush, Moz
- Content Platforms: WordPress, Medium
- AI Tools for Content Creation: ChatGPT, Grammarly, Canva
- Educational Materials: Online courses on AI and content creation from platforms like Coursera, Udemy, and edX
- Community Forums: Engage with other users to share experiences and tips on platforms like Reddit's r/OpenAI and LinkedIn Groups

Chapter 4: Strategy 2 – Streaming Customer Service

Enhancing Customer Support with ChatGPT

In the dynamic landscape of customer service and support, ChatGPT emerges as a game-changer. With its advanced capabilities, ChatGPT can significantly enhance how businesses interact with and support their customers. However, adopting ChatGPT requires a strategic approach to ensure effective integration without overestimating its capabilities or rushing the implementation process.

Stat Insight: According to a 2022 Zendesk poll, 50% of businesses believe their cross-functional teams understand AI's current capabilities. This growing awareness highlights the importance of leveraging AI to meet and exceed customer expectations.

Businesses harnessing AI effectively can improve customer retention and acquisition by gaining deeper insights into customer needs and preferences. Language learning models like ChatGPT enable firms to refine their customer service methods, enhancing efficiency and effectiveness. Prioritizing excellent customer service ensures customers feel valued and satisfied, leading to long-term loyalty and positive business outcomes.

1. Accelerate the Onboarding Process

Streamlining Onboarding with ChatGPT

Remember the old days of onboarding when you had to juggle multiple AI solutions like a circus performer with too many balls? ChatGPT has stepped in to save the day, transforming the process entirely. At the same time, previous AI tools had limitations; finding the right balance and making the most of what we have is essential—much like pairing a fine wine with cheese.

Benefits:

- Relevance and Contextualization: ChatGPT makes customer service more relevant and contextual, which is essential for effective business operations.
- Streamlined Support: Enables specialized teams to streamline customer support, accelerating and enhancing the engagement process.

Fun Fact: According to a McKinsey report, companies that successfully adopt AI improve their business processes by up to 30%.

Case Study: Acme Corp

- Challenge: High onboarding time and low new hire satisfaction.
- Solution: Integrated ChatGPT into their onboarding process.
- Results: Achieved a 40% reduction in onboarding time. New hires reported higher satisfaction levels due to the streamlined and personalized onboarding experience.

Action Step: Implement ChatGPT in your onboarding process to provide new employees instant access to information, personalized training materials, and support, reducing onboarding time and improving satisfaction.

Reflection Prompt: How can accelerating your onboarding process with ChatGPT improve your team's overall productivity and satisfaction?

2. Provide Multiple Potential Answers

Enhancing Responsiveness with ChatGPT

ChatGPT doesn't just spit out answers; it crafts responses with the finesse of a seasoned diplomat. It simulates human replies, striving to comprehend questions and provide personalized responses. This capability is invaluable for businesses aiming to communicate with customers more conversationally.

Benefits:

- Human-Like Interactions: Creates a more engaging and relatable customer experience.
- Personalization: Tailor's responses to individual customer needs, enhancing satisfaction.

Case Study: Tech Solutions Inc.

- Challenge: Low customer satisfaction due to slow and generic responses.
- Solution: Utilized ChatGPT to handle customer inquiries.
- Results: Achieved a 25% increase in customer satisfaction scores. Customers appreciated the quick and accurate responses, feeling their issues were understood and addressed promptly.

Tip: Understanding how prompts maximize ChatGPT's effectiveness is like knowing how to cook a perfect steak—a foundational skill for success.

Action Step: Train your customer support team to use specific and clear prompts with ChatGPT to generate accurate and personalized responses.

Reflection Prompt: Think about a recent customer interaction. How could ChatGPT have made it more efficient and engaging?

3. Categorize Questions and Queries

Optimizing Support with ChatGPT

Customer support personnel often spend significant time sorting and categorizing questions. Enter ChatGPT, the organizational wizard! It quickly organizes and groups information, revolutionizing efficiency and process optimization.

Benefits:

- Efficiency: Reduces the effort required by customer support staff.
- Consistency: Ensures consistent responses across various scenarios.

Humorous Anecdote: Imagine if Sherlock Holmes had ChatGPT to categorize clues. Watson would have been out of a job!

Action Step: Implement ChatGPT to automatically categorize incoming customer queries by topic, urgency, or department, ensuring they are swiftly directed to the appropriate team.

Reflection Prompt: How can automating the categorization of customer queries with ChatGPT improve your support team's efficiency and response times?

4. Summarize Long Conversations

Streamlining Communication with ChatGPT

ChatGPT can summarize lengthy conversations, articles, blog posts, research papers, or white papers. Think of it as the TL;DR hero we all need! Businesses should also shorten lengthy client dialogues to increase interest and engagement.

Benefits:

- Clarity: Provides clear, concise information.
- Time-Saving: Enables businesses to serve more customers efficiently.

Case Study: Global Enterprises

- Challenge: Long customer service chats lead to delayed follow-ups.
- Solution: Used ChatGPT to summarize lengthy customer service conversations.
- Results: Achieved a 30% reduction in follow-up times. Customers received clear summaries of their issues and the steps taken to resolve them, enhancing their overall experience.

Action Step: Utilize ChatGPT to generate summaries of customer interactions, helping your team quickly grasp the core issues and expedite resolutions.

Reflection Prompt: How can summarizing long customer conversations with ChatGPT enhance your team's ability to address issues promptly and effectively?

5. Proactively Engage and Help

Boosting Responsiveness with ChatGPT

AI-powered customer service solutions like ChatGPT can help businesses respond to customers faster. In business, time is everything—just ask any New Yorker trying to catch a cab. Customers feel more at ease asking questions if they receive responses in seconds.

Benefits:

- Speed: Provides instant responses, enhancing customer satisfaction.
- Engagement: Keeps customers engaged by addressing their needs proactively.

Fun Fact: Studies show that 75% of consumers expect a response within five minutes of contacting customer service online.

Action Step: Integrate ChatGPT into your customer support system to provide real-time assistance, reduce wait times, and improve overall customer satisfaction.

Reflection Prompt: How can proactively engaging with customers using ChatGPT improve their overall experience and loyalty to your brand?

6. Track Overall Customer Support and Service Quality

Monitoring Excellence with ChatGPT

Customer service and support concerns are widespread in enterprises. ChatGPT and other AI-based solutions are revolutionizing customer delight and service quality monitoring. They allow businesses to track customer needs and expectations accurately, like having a virtual assistant.

Benefits:

- Insightful Analytics: Identifies areas for improvement through data analysis.
- Consistency: Ensures consistent service quality across all interactions.

Visual Element Suggestion: To demonstrate the improvement visually, include a chart showing customer satisfaction scores before and after implementing ChatGPT.

Action Step: Use ChatGPT to analyze customer support conversations and generate reports highlighting key metrics and areas for enhancement.

Reflection Prompt: How can tracking and analyzing customer support interactions with ChatGPT help you identify and address service gaps?

7. Increasing Customer Satisfaction and Retention

Enhancing Loyalty with ChatGPT

AI technologies have advanced significantly over the last decade, particularly in business. ChatGPT is setting the standard in this digital age. Companies can use advanced language learning models like ChatGPT to improve customer satisfaction and retention.

Benefits:

- Personalized Experiences: Tailors interactions to individual customer preferences.
- Efficiency: Provides timely and accurate responses, reducing frustration and increasing satisfaction.

Case Study: Retail Giant

- Challenge: Low customer retention rates despite high initial sales.
- Solution: Integrated ChatGPT with their CRM system.
- Results: Achieved a 20% increase in customer retention rates. Personalized interactions and timely responses made customers feel valued and appreciated.

Action Step: Integrate ChatGPT with your CRM to provide personalized interactions, enhancing customer loyalty and retention.

Reflection Prompt: How can personalized customer interactions with ChatGPT foster long-term loyalty and improve retention rates?

8. Personalize Your Customer Experience (CX)

Tailoring Interactions with ChatGPT

AI is beneficial for organizations dealing with complex client data. It allows them to gain insights that help them make informed decisions. Gathering information about clients' interests, purchases, and interactions helps create AI chatbot solutions tailored to each customer.

Benefits:

- Customization: Delivers personalized experiences based on individual customer data.
- Engagement: Increases customer engagement by addressing specific needs and preferences.

Action Step: Use ChatGPT to analyze customer data and generate personalized recommendations, enhancing the overall customer experience.

Reflection Prompt: How can personalizing customer interactions with ChatGPT improve engagement and satisfaction?

9. Integrate AI-Based Chatbots

Seamless Support with ChatGPT

Including an AI chatbot in your mobile app and company website increases customer happiness and retention. Direct consumer touch is critical for your company, simplifying the process of asking questions and receiving help.

Benefits:

- 24/7 Availability: Provides support outside of regular business hours.
- Consistency: Ensures uniform responses across different platforms.

Action Step: Deploy ChatGPT-powered chatbots on your website and mobile app to offer instant customer support and assistance.

Reflection Prompt: How can integrating ChatGPT-based chatbots across multiple platforms enhance your customers' support experience?

10. Train Your AI Chatbot

Ensuring Accuracy with ChatGPT

Beyond implementing an AI-powered chatbot, businesses should ensure it understands their business and target audience. This enables it to provide accurate and helpful answers. Training an AI chatbot with internal data improves its responses.

Benefits:

- Relevance: Provides responses aligned with your business's specific needs and context.
- Accuracy: Reduces the likelihood of incorrect or irrelevant answers.

Action Step: Train ChatGPT with your company's data, FAQs, and customer interactions to enhance its understanding and response accuracy.

Reflection Prompt: How can regularly training your ChatGPT chatbot with internal data improve its effectiveness and reliability?

11. Provide Omni-Channel Support

Consistent Service Across Platforms with ChatGPT

AI chatbots are transforming customer service across channels. Being available on multiple channels ensures a consistent customer experience. Support customers wherever they are, whether through messaging apps, phone calls, or email. This provides a seamless experience across mediums.

Benefits:

- Accessibility: Meets customers on their preferred platforms.
- Consistency: Maintains uniform service quality across all channels.

Humorous Anecdote: Imagine if Batman had an AI chatbot to handle Alfred's calls. Gotham would be even safer!

Action Step: Implement ChatGPT across all your customer service channels to provide a unified and consistent support experience.

Reflection Prompt: How can offering omni-channel support with ChatGPT improve your customers' overall experience and satisfaction?

12. Expand Understanding of Natural Language Processing (NLP)

Enhancing Communication with ChatGPT

Businesses should harness Natural Language Processing (NLP) to address client concerns better. Learning NLP helps provide accurate answers to customers' questions. Developing user-friendly strategies to engage customers ensures a consistent experience across all touchpoints.

Benefits:

- Improved Comprehension: Better understanding of customer queries and intent.
- Enhanced Interaction: More natural and effective communication.

Action Step: Invest in training or resources to deepen your team's understanding of NLP and its applications in customer service with ChatGPT.

Reflection Prompt: How could understanding NLP enhance your business's customer service interactions?

13. Common Challenges and Solutions in AI-Driven Customer Service

While ChatGPT offers numerous advantages in customer service, integrating it into existing systems and workflows can present challenges. Proactively addressing these obstacles ensures you can harness AI effectively without compromising quality or integrity.

Common Challenges:

1. Maintaining Originality and Avoiding Plagiarism:
   - Challenge: AI-generated responses may inadvertently mimic existing content, leading to potential plagiarism issues.
   - Solution: Always review and edit AI-generated content to infuse your unique voice and ensure originality. Use plagiarism detection tools like Grammarly or Copyscape to verify content uniqueness.
2. Ensuring Content Accuracy:
   - Challenge: AI may produce information that needs to be updated or corrected.

- Solution: Implement a rigorous fact-checking process. Cross-reference AI outputs with reliable sources and update data regularly to maintain accuracy.

3. Balancing AI Assistance with Human Creativity:

    - Challenge: Over-reliance on AI can result in generic or less engaging content.

    - Solution: Use AI as a starting point for ideas and drafts, then refine and enhance the content with your creativity and insights to make it more engaging and personalized.

4. Managing SEO and Readability:

    - Challenge: AI might prioritize SEO over readability, leading to search-engine-optimized content that is difficult for readers to engage with.

    - Solution: Balance SEO best practices with natural language and readability. Use AI to assist with SEO elements, but ensure the final content is reader-friendly by editing for flow and clarity.

5. Handling Sensitive Topics:

    - Challenge: AI may generate inappropriate or insensitive content and susceptible subjects.

    - Solution: Carefully review AI-generated content on sensitive topics. Implement guidelines and ethical standards to ensure respectful and accurate representation.

6. Integration with Existing Workflows:

    - Challenge: Incorporating AI tools into established customer service workflows can be disruptive.

    - Solution: Gradually integrate AI tools by starting with specific tasks (e.g., categorizing queries or drafting responses) and expanding their use as you become more comfortable. Provide training and resources to your team to facilitate smooth adoption.

Best Practices to Overcome Challenges:

1. Establish Clear Guidelines:

    - Define how and when to use AI to maintain consistency and quality in your customer service process.

2. Continuous Training:

    - Stay updated with AI developments and train your team to use AI tools effectively.

3. Feedback Loops:

    - Create mechanisms for regular feedback on AI-generated content to identify areas for improvement and adjust strategies accordingly.

4. Human Oversight:

    - Ensure all AI-generated content undergo human review to maintain standards and promptly address issues.

5. Technical Integration:

    - Use APIs and integration tools to integrate ChatGPT into your existing customer service platforms seamlessly. Tools like Zapier or Salesforce Einstein can facilitate this integration.

6. Data Privacy and Security:

    - Implement robust data privacy measures to protect customer information. Ensure that ChatGPT interactions comply with relevant data protection regulations, such as GDPR or CCPA.

Case Study: Overcoming AI Challenges at HealthPlus Blog HealthPlus Blog integrated ChatGPT into their customer service process to streamline article drafting. Initially, they faced issues with maintaining originality and ensuring content accuracy. They enhanced content uniqueness and reliability by implementing a strict review process and using plagiarism detection tools. Additionally, they trained their writers to refine AI drafts with personal insights, resulting in more engaging and trustworthy articles. This balanced approach led to a 30% increase in reader engagement and a significant boost in search engine rankings.

Action Step: Identify the challenges in your customer service process and develop strategies using AI tools to address them effectively.

Reflection Prompt: What potential challenges might you encounter when integrating AI into your customer service, and how can you proactively address them to ensure success?

Conclusion: Transforming Customer Service with ChatGPT

Enhancing customer service with ChatGPT is not just about adopting new technology but transforming the customer experience. Businesses can provide faster, more accurate, and personalized support by strategically integrating AI, boosting customer satisfaction and loyalty. As AI continues to evolve, the opportunities for improving customer service are boundless. Use ChatGPT wisely, combine it effectively, and watch your customer service soar to new heights.

Key Takeaways:

- AI is a Tool, Not a Replacement: Combine AI capabilities with human creativity and empathy.
- Quality Over Quantity: Focus on creating valuable and engaging interactions.
- Ethics Matter: Uphold transparency, integrity, and fairness in all AI-assisted customer service endeavors.
- Strategic Integration: Implement ChatGPT thoughtfully to maximize benefits and ensure seamless integration with existing systems.

Call to Action: Start exploring how ChatGPT can assist in your customer service journey today. Experiment with integrating AI chatbots, personalizing interactions, and leveraging AI for proactive engagement. By embracing these strategies, you're positioning your business to lead and succeed in the rapidly advancing world of AI-driven customer service.

Engagement Exercise

Action Item: Choose a customer service process in your business and use ChatGPT to assist with a component, such as drafting responses, categorizing queries, or summarizing conversations.

Reflect: Assess the quality of ChatGPT's output. What worked well? What needed adjustment? How did it enhance your productivity and customer satisfaction?

Example: If you're managing a help desk, ask ChatGPT to generate responses for common technical issues. Evaluate how these responses compare to your current solutions and implement improvements based on the feedback.

Additional Resources:

- AI Integration Tools: Zapier, HubSpot, Salesforce Einstein
- NLP Learning Platforms: Coursera NLP Courses, edX NLP Programs
- Community Forums: Engage with other users on platforms like Reddit's r/OpenAI and LinkedIn Groups
- Ethical AI Guidelines: OpenAI's Responsible AI

Chapter 5: Strategy 3 – Scaling Social Media Management

Automating Social Media Posts with ChatGPT

Imagine if your business could automate social media updates and create a plethora of content across multiple platforms without breaking a sweat. Sounds like a dream, right? Well, wake up and smell the AI—because ChatGPT is here to make that dream a reality!

Some people feel startups and small businesses don't need social media professionals. Sure, but why hire a full-time juggler when you have a circus-performing AI? ChatGPT helps startups and small companies streamline their social media marketing, saving time and money while boosting their online presence. It's like having a marketing team that never sleeps.

Fun Fact: According to a survey by Buffer, 73% of marketers believe that social media marketing has been effective or very practical for their business.

1. Creating Engaging Content with ChatGPT

Imagine if your business could whip up engaging content as effortlessly as a magician pulls rabbits out of hats. That's what ChatGPT does for social media influencers, entrepreneurs, and business owners. It's their secret weapon for creating captivating and innovative material, enhancing online visibility and audience engagement.

Benefits:

- Efficiency: Reduces the time spent on drafting and editing posts.
- Creativity: Generates fresh ideas and diverse content formats.
- Consistency: Maintains a steady flow of content across all platforms.

Example:

- Prompt: "Create five engaging Instagram captions for a sustainable fashion brand promoting eco-friendly materials."

Action Step: Use ChatGPT to generate a week's social media captions. Review and customize them to align with your brand's voice and message.

Reflection Prompt: How can diversifying your social media content with ChatGPT improve audience engagement and brand loyalty?

2. Automating and Optimizing Social Media

Have you ever considered using Hootsuite to manage your social media accounts? Think of ChatGPT as Hootsuite's clever sibling. It helps automate posts and ensures they're optimized for maximum engagement. This AI marvel helps businesses attract attention, raise brand awareness, and engage their target audience like never before.

Benefits:

- Time-Saving: Automates repetitive tasks, freeing up your schedule for strategic planning.
- Optimization: Tailors content for each platform's unique algorithms and audience preferences.
- Scalability: Easily manage multiple accounts and campaigns simultaneously.

Case Study: Startup X

- Challenge: Managing multiple social media accounts with limited resources.
- Solution: Integrated ChatGPT will automate post-creation and scheduling.
- Results: Increased social media engagement by 35% and reduced management time by 50%.

Use platform-specific prompts to generate content tailored to each social media channel. For example, create more professional LinkedIn content and casual Instagram posts.

Action Step: Develop a content calendar using ChatGPT to plan and schedule posts across all your social media platforms for the upcoming month.

Reflection Prompt: How could automating your social media tasks free up more time for other critical business activities?

3. Enhancing Social Media Consistency

Have you ever struggled to keep your brand's voice consistent across Facebook, Instagram, Twitter, and other platforms? ChatGPT has you covered. It helps businesses communicate swiftly and consistently, ensuring your brand message hits the mark every time.

Benefits:

- Uniform Messaging: Maintains a consistent tone and style across all platforms.

- Brand Integrity: Strengthens brand identity by ensuring all content aligns with your core values and messaging.
- Efficiency: Reduces the effort required to tailor content for each platform manually.

Example:

- Prompt: "Create a consistent brand message for a tech startup focusing on innovative solutions and customer-centric services."
- ChatGPT Response: "At [Startup Name], we revolutionize the tech landscape with innovative solutions tailored to your unique needs. Our customer-centric approach ensures that you receive unparalleled support and cutting-edge technology to drive your success."

Action Step: Use ChatGPT to draft a brand messaging guide that outlines your tone, style, and key messages to ensure consistency across all social media platforms.

Reflection Prompt: How can maintaining a consistent brand voice across social media platforms improve your brand's recognition and trustworthiness?

4. Building a Powerful Online Presence

Building a solid and engaging online presence takes time and effort, even with ChatGPT in your toolkit. It's like planting a garden—you need to nurture it, water it, and sometimes talk to your plants (or, in this case, your audience). Remember, a little effort goes a long way.

Benefits:

- Increased Visibility: Regular, high-quality posts enhance your brand's online presence.
- Audience Engagement: Engaging content fosters a loyal and interactive community.
- Business Growth: A robust online presence attracts new customers and drives conversions.

Think of ChatGPT as your digital gardener—except it doesn't mind getting its hands dirty with algorithms.

Action Step: Develop a comprehensive social media strategy using ChatGPT to create diverse content types (e.g., posts, stories, reels) that engage your audience and build your online presence.

Reflection Prompt: How can a strong and consistent online presence impact your business's growth and customer loyalty?

5. Search Engine Optimization (SEO)

In the digital age, SEO is the holy grail. ChatGPT can help you achieve SEO nirvana by generating unique content variations that increase user interaction and business conversions. It's like having an SEO guru at your fingertips, guiding you to the top of search engine rankings.

Benefits:

- Improved Rankings: Optimized content boosts your website's visibility on search engines.
- Increased Traffic: Higher rankings lead to more organic traffic and potential customers.
- Enhanced Content Quality: SEO-focused content attracts and retains readers, improving engagement metrics.

Example:

- Prompt: "Generate SEO-friendly hashtags for a post about eco-friendly home products."
- ChatGPT Response: "#EcoFriendlyLiving #SustainableHome #GreenProducts #EcoConscious #ZeroWasteHome #SustainableLiving #GreenHome #EcoFriendlyProducts #EnvironmentallyFriendly #SustainableLifestyle"

Action Step: Use ChatGPT to generate SEO-optimized content, including meta titles, descriptions, and hashtags, to enhance your social media posts and improve search engine rankings.

Reflection Prompt: How can integrating ChatGPT with your SEO strategy improve your website's visibility and traffic?

6. Brand Identification and Recognition

What do all businesses crave? A solid social media presence, of course! ChatGPT helps companies enhance their brand identity and recognition by ensuring consistency across all platforms. Once customers engage with your brand, they will know it anywhere, creating a loyal following.

Benefits:

- Enhanced Brand Identity: Consistent messaging and visuals strengthen brand recognition.
- Increased Trust: A recognizable and consistent brand fosters customer trust and loyalty.
- Competitive Advantage: Strong brand recognition differentiates your business from competitors.

Fun Fact: According to Nielsen, 92% of consumers trust recommendations from people they know over other forms of advertising.

Action Step: Use ChatGPT to develop a brand style guide that outlines your brand's voice, tone, and visual elements to ensure consistency across all social media channels.

Reflection Prompt: How can enhancing your brand identity and recognition through ChatGPT influence customer loyalty and business growth?

7. User Experience (UX)

User experience is more than improving online shopping—it's about creating memorable interactions on social media platforms. ChatGPT helps provide a consistent user experience across all your platforms, making it easy for users to connect with your brand.

Benefits:

- Enhanced Interactions: Provides meaningful and engaging interactions with your audience.
- Streamlined Communication: Facilitates clear and efficient communication, reducing misunderstandings.
- Increased Engagement: Memorable interactions encourage repeat visits and ongoing engagement.

Imagine if your social media was as responsive as a chatty barista who never forgets your favorite order. That's the kind of user experience ChatGPT aims to create.

Action Step: Implement ChatGPT to manage and respond to social media interactions, ensuring a consistent and positive user experience across all platforms.

Reflection Prompt: How can providing a consistent and engaging user experience with ChatGPT improve your brand's reputation and customer loyalty?

Conclusion: Scaling Social Media Management with ChatGPT

Scaling social media management with ChatGPT is like having a magic wand for your marketing efforts. It automates, optimizes, and personalizes your content, freeing you to focus on what truly matters—building meaningful connections with your audience. As AI continues to evolve, the possibilities for enhancing social media management are endless.

Ultimately, it's not just about the number of posts but the quality of interactions. Let ChatGPT help you create social media magic that leaves a lasting impression.

Key Takeaways:

- AI is a Tool, Not a Replacement: Combine AI capabilities with human creativity and empathy.

- Quality Over Quantity: Focus on creating valuable and engaging interactions.
- Ethics Matter: Uphold transparency, integrity, and fairness in all AI-assisted customer service endeavors.
- Strategic Integration: Implement ChatGPT thoughtfully to maximize benefits and ensure seamless integration with existing systems.

Action Steps:

1. Implement AI Tools: To streamline your social media workflow, start using ChatGPT for brainstorming, content creation, and scheduling.
2. Optimize for SEO: Utilize ChatGPT to enhance your social media posts with SEO-friendly keywords and hashtags.
3. Monetize Thoughtfully: Explore and integrate monetization strategies that align with your content and audience needs.
4. Maintain Ethical Standards: Establish guidelines to ensure your AI-generated content remains accurate, original, and unbiased.
5. Continuous Learning: Stay updated with AI advancements and refine your social media management strategies.

Reflection Prompt:

Consider a recent content project you worked on. How could AI have improved your process? Reflect on balancing AI assistance and your creative input to enhance efficiency and quality.

Additional Resources:

- AI Integration Tools: Zapier, HubSpot, Salesforce Einstein
- NLP Learning Platforms: Coursera NLP Courses, edX NLP Programs
- Community Forums: Engage with other users on platforms like Reddit's r/OpenAI and LinkedIn Groups
- Ethical AI Guidelines: OpenAI's Responsible AI Practices

Chapter 6: Strategy 4 – Expanding E-commerce Capabilities

AI-Generated Product Descriptions and Reviews: Crafting Compelling Content with ChatGPT

ChatGPT has taken the business world by storm, and for good reason! E-commerce companies used to rely on AI for product descriptions, but ChatGPT takes it to the next level. Now, you can craft descriptions and reviews that inform, engage, and entertain.

Imagine running an e-commerce site with tons of products to describe. Writing each description manually feels like swimming in an ocean of words. Enter ChatGPT. This helper can quickly whip up product descriptions, and they're perfect.

Example:

- Before ChatGPT: "This is a red t-shirt made of cotton."
- After ChatGPT: "Rock your style with this vibrant red t-shirt, made from soft, breathable cotton. Perfect for any casual outing!"

Businesses love ChatGPT because it saves time and money, creating unique, appealing content that grabs customers' attention. No more spending hours writing descriptions—just plug in your details and let ChatGPT do its magic.

The Importance of Good Product Descriptions and Reviews: Elevating Your Sales Game

Product descriptions and reviews can make or break a sale. A good description highlights features, benefits, and unique selling points, acting like a virtual sales associate.

Example:

- Basic Description: "A 12-cup coffee maker."
- Enhanced with ChatGPT: "Wake up to the aroma of freshly brewed coffee with our 12-cup coffee maker. It's easy to use and has programmable settings that let you enjoy your perfect cup every morning. Your mornings just got better!"

Reviews build trust and can convince hesitant buyers to buy. ChatGPT can generate realistic, positive reviews that highlight the best aspects of your products, boosting sales.

Leveraging Data: Real-life Examples and Statistical Insights

Let's look at some case studies to illustrate the impact of AI-generated content. A survey by [Industry Expert Group] revealed that businesses using AI-generated product descriptions experienced a 20% increase in conversion rates within six months of implementation. This demonstrates the benefits of integrating AI tools like ChatGPT into e-commerce strategies.

Case Study: EcoGoods Online

- Challenge: Low conversion rates due to unengaging product descriptions.
- Solution: Implemented ChatGPT to generate compelling product descriptions.
- Results: Saw a 25% increase in conversion rates and a 15% boost in average order value.

Fun Fact: According to a survey by Buffer, 73% of marketers believe that social media marketing has been effective or very practical for their business.

Embracing AI Tools Like Jasper and CopyAI: Expanding Your Arsenal

Other AI tools are worth mentioning besides ChatGPT. Jasper is fantastic for generating concise and attractive product descriptions. ChatGPT might be less advanced than it is, but it does the job efficiently. With Grammarly integration, your descriptions will be error-free and professional.

CopyAI offers versatility and speed in generating marketing content. It can produce multiple content pieces simultaneously, saving time and resources while maintaining consistency across marketing efforts. Plus, being free to use, CopyAI is a cost-effective solution for startups and small businesses.

Comparison Table: ChatGPT vs. Jasper vs. CopyAI

Best Tips and Practices for Using AI Tools Effectively

1. Experiment with Different Tools:
    - Don't limit yourself to just one AI tool. Explore various platforms like ChatGPT, Jasper, and CopyAI to find the best fit for your needs.
2. Customize Outputs:
    - Tailor AI-generated content to align with your brand voice and style. Add personal touches to make the content unique and engaging.
3. Stay Updated:

- Keep abreast of advancements in AI technology and platform updates. Regularly check for new features that can enhance your content creation process.

4. Combine AI with Human Creativity:

    - Use AI-generated content as a foundation and add your unique perspective to make it stand out.

5. Monitor Performance:

    - Track metrics like engagement rates, conversion rates, and customer feedback to refine your approach and improve the effectiveness of your content.

Analyzing Data for Insights and Optimization

Incorporate data analysis into your content creation process to gain actionable insights and optimize your strategies. Utilize tools like Google Analytics, social media insights, and customer feedback to understand audience preferences and refine your content.

Example:

- Prompt: "Analyze the performance of our latest product descriptions and suggest improvements."

- ChatGPT Response: "Based on the data, your product descriptions with emotional appeals have higher engagement rates. Consider incorporating more emotional language and customer-centric benefits to further boost conversions."

Action Step: Review your content performance data regularly and use ChatGPT to generate suggestions for optimization based on the insights gathered.

Reflection Prompt: How can data-driven insights from ChatGPT improve your content strategies and drive better business outcomes?

Scaling Your Content Creation Efforts

As your business grows, scaling your content creation becomes essential. Use AI tools to maintain consistency and efficiency while scaling content production to meet increasing demand. Automate repetitive tasks and streamline workflows, allowing you to focus on strategic initiatives and growth.

Benefits:

- Consistency: Ensures uniform quality and tone across all content pieces.

- Efficiency: Handles high volumes of content creation without compromising quality.

- Scalability: Easily scales content production to match business growth and market demands.

Action Step: Develop a scalable content strategy using ChatGPT to manage increased content needs and ensure consistency and quality as your business expands.

Reflection Prompt: How can scaling your content creation with ChatGPT support your business's growth and market presence?

Exploring Emerging Technologies in E-commerce

Stay ahead by exploring emerging technologies that complement AI in e-commerce. From Augmented Reality (AR) for immersive shopping experiences to Blockchain for secure transactions, integrating cutting-edge technologies can enhance the customer journey and differentiate your brand.

Example:

- AR Integration: Use AR to allow customers to visualize products in their environment, increasing engagement and reducing return rates.

- Blockchain for Security: Implement blockchain technology to ensure secure and transparent transactions, building customer trust.

Action Step: Research and pilot emerging technologies that can complement your AI-driven e-commerce strategies, enhancing overall customer experience and operational efficiency.

Reflection Prompt: What emerging technologies can you integrate with ChatGPT to further enhance your e-commerce capabilities and customer experience?

Continuous Learning and Adaptation

In the rapidly evolving field of e-commerce, continuous learning and adaptation are essential. Invest in education and training to keep pace with industry trends, technological advancements, and changing consumer behaviors.

Benefits:

- Staying Competitive: Keeps your strategies up-to-date with the latest market trends and technologies.

- Innovation: Encourages the adoption of new ideas and approaches to enhance business operations.

- Adaptability: Prepares your business to respond to changes in the market and consumer preferences quickly.

Action Step: Enroll in online courses on AI and e-commerce, attend webinars, and participate in industry forums to stay informed and continuously refine your strategies.

Reflection Prompt: How can committing to continuous learning and adaptation ensure your e-commerce strategies remain effective and competitive?

Conclusion: Harnessing the Power of AI for E-commerce Success

By embracing AI tools like ChatGPT, Jasper, and CopyAI, leveraging data for insights, scaling content creation efforts, exploring emerging technologies, and prioritizing continuous learning, you can unlock AI's full potential for e-commerce success. Embrace innovation, experiment boldly, and stay agile to thrive in the dynamic world of online commerce.

Key Takeaways:

- AI is a Tool, Not a Replacement: Combine AI capabilities with human creativity to produce compelling and authentic content.
- Quality Over Quantity: Focus on creating valuable, engaging interactions that resonate with your audience.
- Ethics Matter: Uphold transparency, integrity, and fairness in all AI-assisted content creation endeavors.
- Strategic Integration: Implement ChatGPT thoughtfully to maximize benefits and ensure seamless integration with existing systems.
- Continuous Learning: Stay updated with AI advancements and refine your content creation strategies.

Action Steps:

1. Implement AI Tools:
    - To streamline your e-commerce workflow, start using ChatGPT, Jasper, and CopyAI for brainstorming, content creation, and scheduling.
2. Optimize for SEO:
    - Utilize ChatGPT to enhance your product descriptions with SEO-friendly keywords and hashtags.
3. Monetize Thoughtfully:
    - Explore and integrate monetization strategies that align with your content and audience needs.

4. Maintain Ethical Standards:
    - Establish guidelines to ensure your AI-generated content remains accurate, original, and unbiased.
5. Continuous Learning:
    - Stay updated with AI advancements and continuously refine your e-commerce strategies to stay competitive.

Reflection Prompt:

Consider a recent content project you worked on. How could AI have improved your process? Reflect on balancing AI assistance and your creative input to enhance efficiency and quality.

Chapter 7: Strategy 5 – Personalized Marketing Campaigns

Creating Tailored Marketing Messages with AI

Imagine you're running a small bakery, sending out generic emails about your latest cupcake flavors. Your customers, bombarded with impersonal ads daily, barely give them a second glance.

Now, picture this: your emails are tailored to each customer's taste, mentioning their favorite flavors and suggesting new ones based on past orders. Suddenly, your engagement skyrockets, and your loyal customers feel even more connected to your brand.

That's the magic of personalized marketing with AI!

Absolutely! AI tools like ChatGPT are becoming indispensable in delivering customized marketing messages. Exciting, right? But let's face it, using ChatGPT for personalized marketing can seem as complicated as assembling IKEA furniture without instructions.

Fortunately, more people are learning ChatGPT prompts and finding ways to simplify the process. Whether through Chrome extensions or native applications, ChatGPT offers countless ways to create intelligent and personalized communications. It's like having a marketing wizard at your fingertips.

1. Segmenting Your Audience

Understanding Your Audience for Targeted Messaging

Start by segmenting your target audience. Understand who they are, what they like, and what problems they need solving. This knowledge allows you to tailor your messaging to their needs and desires, making your marketing more effective. Think of it as creating a personalized playlist for each of your customers—one that hits all the right notes.

Benefits:

- Enhanced Relevance: Tailored messages resonate more deeply with each segment.
- Increased Engagement: Targeted content is more likely to capture attention and inspire action.

Example:

- Prompt: "Segment our customer base for a fashion e-commerce store based on purchase history and preferences."
- ChatGPT Response:

  a. Frequent Shoppers: Customers who make multiple purchases monthly and are interested in the latest trends.

  b. Bargain Hunters: Customers who respond well to discounts and promotions.

  c. Premium Buyers: Customers who prefer high-end, exclusive products.

  d. Seasonal Shoppers: Customers who purchase items based on seasons or holidays.

Case Study: Boutique Bliss

- Challenge: Low engagement rates due to generic marketing messages.
- Solution: Utilized ChatGPT to segment their audience based on purchase behavior and preferences.
- Results: Increased email open rates by 35% and conversion rates by 20%.

Action Step: Use ChatGPT to analyze customer data and create detailed audience segments. Tailor your marketing campaigns to address each segment's specific needs and preferences.

Reflection Prompt: How can segmenting your audience with ChatGPT improve the effectiveness of your marketing campaigns and drive higher engagement?

2. Boosting Conversion Rates and ROI

Enhancing Sales with AI-Driven Strategies

Professional salespeople use ChatGPT and other AI-powered tools to boost conversions and ROI. ChatGPT can help sales teams increase conversion rates by optimizing various funnel elements.

a. Shorten Conversion Time

Streamlining the Sales Process

One of ChatGPT's most valuable applications is speeding up conversions. Average consumers often struggle with forms, so they don't complete transactions.

How ChatGPT Helps:

- Simplifying Forms: Distinguishes between relevant and irrelevant fields, merging the best ones to make form filling easier.

- Filtering Entries: Filters required entries to reduce the average user's form-filling time.
- Options Comparison: Expedites the process of comparing products or services, aiding quick decision-making.

Case Study: FastTrack Electronics

- Challenge: High abandonment rates during the checkout process.
- Solution: Implemented ChatGPT to simplify and optimize the checkout forms.
- Results: Reduced form-filling time by 25%, leading to a 15% increase in completed transactions.

Action Step: Use ChatGPT to analyze and optimize your checkout forms, making them more user-friendly and reducing abandonment rates.

Reflection Prompt: How can shortening your conversion process with ChatGPT enhance your sales efficiency and customer satisfaction?

b. Add Great CTAs

Crafting Compelling Call-to-Actions

When crafting great CTAs, the possibilities are endless. You can use your creativity to build several intuitive and appealing CTAs that will resonate with your target audience and help grow your business. ChatGPT speeds up this process by generating a comprehensive list of personalized CTAs in seconds. It's a significant shift for firms looking to optimize their marketing techniques.

Benefits:

- Creativity Boost: Generates diverse and innovative CTAs.
- Personalization: Tailors CTAs to specific business needs and audience preferences.

Example:

- Prompt: "Create five compelling CTAs for a landing page promoting eco-friendly water bottles."
- ChatGPT Response:

  a. "Join the Green Movement Today!"

  b. "Get Your Eco-Friendly Bottle Now!"

  c. "Make a Sustainable Choice – Shop Now!"

  d. "Stay Hydrated and Save the Planet!"

  e. "Upgrade to Eco-Friendly Hydration!"

Case Study: GreenSip

- Challenge: Low engagement with existing CTAs.
- Solution: Utilized ChatGPT to generate a variety of personalized CTAs.
- Results: Increased click-through rates by 30% and boosted sales by 20%.

Tip: Use ChatGPT to generate multiple CTAs and A/B test them to determine which resonates best with your audience.

Action Step: Using ChatGPT, develop a list of personalized CTAs and implement A/B testing to identify the most effective ones for your campaigns.

Reflection Prompt: How can creating diverse and personalized CTAs with ChatGPT improve your campaign's engagement and conversion rates?

3. Localize Content

Tailoring Marketing for Local Markets

Focus on fine-tuning local content and marketing approaches to boost conversion rates. Creating location-specific content, managing region-specific online listings, and maintaining localized marketing strategies can significantly enhance your reach and relevance.

Benefits:

- Increased Relevance: Localized content resonates more with the target audience.
- Enhanced Trust: Demonstrates understanding of local preferences and needs.

Example:

- Prompt: "Localize our product descriptions for the French market."
- ChatGPT Response: "Découvrez notre bouteille d'eau écologique, conçue pour le style de vie parisien. Fabriquée à partir de matériaux durables, elle est parfaite pour vos promenades en ville et vos déplacements quotidiens."

Case Study: ParisianPaws

- Challenge: Limited engagement from French-speaking customers.
- Solution: ChatGPT was used to localize their marketing content for the French market.
- Results: Saw a 40% increase in engagement from French-speaking audiences and a 25% boost in regional sales.

Action Step: Use ChatGPT to create localized content for different regions, ensuring your marketing messages are culturally relevant and engaging.

Reflection Prompt: How can localizing your marketing content with ChatGPT improve your connection with regional audiences and drive sales?

4. Include FAQs Instantly

Enhancing Customer Trust with AI-Generated FAQs

Adding a FAQ section can significantly improve product credibility and customer trust. However, creating comprehensive FAQs often requires extensive research. ChatGPT simplifies this process by quickly generating accurate and relevant FAQs tailored to your products and services.

Benefits:

- Efficiency: Rapidly generates comprehensive FAQs without extensive manual effort.
- Accuracy: Provides well-researched and relevant answers to common customer queries.
- Personalization: Tailors FAQs to address specific customer concerns and interests.

Example:

- Prompt: "Generate five FAQs for our eco-friendly water bottles."
- ChatGPT Response:
    a. Q: "Are your water bottles BPA-free?" A: "Yes, all our water bottles are BPA-free, ensuring safe and healthy hydration."
    b. Q: "How do I clean my eco-friendly water bottle?" A: "You can clean your bottle with warm, soapy water or place it in the dishwasher for easy maintenance."
    c. Q: "What materials are used in your water bottles?" A: "Our bottles are made from durable stainless steel and sustainable bamboo lids."
    d. Q: "Do your water bottles keep beverages cold or hot?" A: "Absolutely! Our insulated bottles can keep your drinks cold for up to 24 hours and hot for up to 12 hours."
    e. Q: "Are your water bottles environmentally friendly?" A: "Our bottles are designed with sustainability in mind, using eco-friendly materials and reusable designs to reduce waste."

Case Study: EcoBottle Co.

- Challenge: Limited time and resources to create comprehensive FAQs.

- Solution: Utilized ChatGPT to generate detailed and relevant FAQs for their product pages.
- Results: Improved customer trust, reduced support inquiries by 20%, and increased sales by 15% due to enhanced product credibility.

Action Step: Use ChatGPT to generate a comprehensive FAQ section for your products or services, addressing common customer queries and concerns.

Reflection Prompt: How can incorporating AI-generated FAQs with ChatGPT enhance your customers' trust and streamline your support processes?

5. Analyzing Data for Insights and Optimization

Leveraging Data for Smarter Marketing Decisions

Incorporate data analysis into your content creation process to gain actionable insights and optimize your strategies. Utilize tools like Google Analytics, social media insights, and customer feedback to understand audience preferences and refine your content.

Benefits:

- Data-Driven Decisions: Makes informed adjustments to marketing strategies based on accurate data.
- Enhanced Performance: Optimizes content to meet audience needs and preferences better.
- Continuous Improvement: Enables ongoing refinement of marketing tactics for better results.

Example:

- Prompt: "Analyze the performance of our latest email marketing campaign and suggest improvements."
- ChatGPT Response: "Based on the data, your email open rates increased by 15%, but click-through rates remained stagnant. Consider enhancing your CTAs by making them more compelling and ensuring they align with the content's value proposition. Additionally, segmenting your audience further could help tailor your messages more effectively."

Action Step: Review your marketing performance data regularly and use ChatGPT to generate suggestions for optimization based on the insights gathered.

Reflection Prompt: How can data-driven insights from ChatGPT improve your marketing strategies and drive better business outcomes?

6. Scaling Your Content Creation Efforts

Maintaining Consistency and Efficiency as You Grow

As your business grows, scaling your content creation becomes essential. Use AI tools to maintain consistency and efficiency while scaling content production to meet increasing demand. Automate repetitive tasks and streamline workflows, allowing you to focus on strategic initiatives and growth.

Benefits:

- Consistency: Ensures uniform quality and tone across all content pieces.
- Efficiency: Handles high volumes of content creation without compromising quality.
- Scalability: Easily scales content production to match business growth and market demands.

Action Step: Develop a scalable content strategy using ChatGPT to manage increased content needs and ensure consistency and quality as your business expands.

Reflection Prompt: How can scaling your content creation with ChatGPT support your business's growth and market presence?

7. Exploring Emerging Technologies in E-commerce

Staying Ahead with Cutting-Edge Innovations

Stay ahead by exploring emerging technologies that complement AI in e-commerce. From Augmented Reality (AR) for immersive shopping experiences to Blockchain for secure transactions, integrating cutting-edge technologies can enhance the customer journey and differentiate your brand.

Benefits:

- Enhanced Customer Experience: Provides innovative and interactive ways for customers to engage with your products.
- Increased Security: Utilizes blockchain for secure and transparent transactions, building customer trust.
- Competitive Advantage: Differentiates your brand by adopting the latest technologies.

Example:

- AR Integration: Use AR to allow customers to visualize products in their environment, increasing engagement and reducing return rates.
- Blockchain for Security: Implement blockchain technology to ensure secure and transparent transactions, building customer trust.

Action Step: Research and pilot emerging technologies that can complement your AI-driven e-commerce strategies, enhancing overall customer experience and operational efficiency.

Reflection Prompt: What emerging technologies can you integrate with ChatGPT to further enhance your e-commerce capabilities and customer experience?

8. Continuous Learning and Adaptation

Adapting to the Evolving E-commerce Landscape

In the rapidly evolving field of e-commerce, continuous learning and adaptation are essential. Invest in education and training to keep pace with industry trends, technological advancements, and changing consumer behaviors.

Benefits:

- Staying Competitive: Keeps your strategies up-to-date with the latest market trends and technologies.
- Innovation: Encourages the adoption of new ideas and approaches to enhance business operations.
- Adaptability: Prepares your business to respond to changes in the market and consumer preferences quickly.

Action Step: Enroll in online courses on AI and e-commerce, attend webinars, and participate in industry forums to stay informed and continuously refine your strategies.

Reflection Prompt: How can committing to continuous learning and adaptation ensure your e-commerce strategies remain effective and competitive?

Conclusion: Harnessing the Power of AI for E-commerce Success

By embracing AI tools like ChatGPT, Jasper, and CopyAI, leveraging data for insights, scaling content creation efforts, exploring emerging technologies, and prioritizing continuous learning, you can unlock AI's full potential for e-commerce success. Embrace innovation, experiment boldly, and stay agile to thrive in the dynamic world of online commerce.

Key Takeaways:

- AI is a Tool, Not a Replacement: Combine AI capabilities with human creativity to produce compelling and authentic content.
- Quality Over Quantity: Focus on creating valuable, engaging interactions that resonate with your audience.
- Ethics Matter: Uphold transparency, integrity, and fairness in all AI-assisted con-

tent creation endeavors.

- Strategic Integration: Implement ChatGPT thoughtfully to maximize benefits and ensure seamless integration with existing systems.
- Continuous Learning: Stay updated with AI advancements and refine your content creation strategies to stay competitive.

Action Steps:

1. Implement AI Tools:
   - To streamline your e-commerce workflow, start using ChatGPT, Jasper, and CopyAI for brainstorming, content creation, and scheduling.
2. Optimize for SEO:
   - Utilize ChatGPT to enhance your product descriptions with SEO-friendly keywords and hashtags.
3. Monetize Thoughtfully:
   - Explore and integrate monetization strategies that align with your content and audience needs.
4. Maintain Ethical Standards:
   - Establish guidelines to ensure your AI-generated content remains accurate, original, and unbiased.
5. Continuous Learning:
   - Stay updated with AI advancements and continuously refine your e-commerce strategies to stay competitive.

Reflection Prompt:

Consider a recent content project you worked on. How could AI have improved your process? Reflect on balancing AI assistance and your creative input to enhance efficiency and quality.

Chapter 8: Strategy 6 - Smart Sales Funnels

Automating Lead Generation and Nurturing

Imagine this: You're a sales professional juggling countless tasks, from lead generation to follow-up emails. It's exhausting, and you wish you had an assistant who could handle it all. Enter AI, the superhero you didn't know you needed.

Automate LinkedIn Lead Generation

If LinkedIn is your playground for generating and nurturing leads, ChatGPT can be your MVP. Imagine having a tool that improves post engagement and boosts conversions. It sounds like a dream, right? With ChatGPT, you can automate responses, generate personalized content, and engage through comments. Consistency is vital, and ChatGPT helps you maintain it, increasing your visibility and enhancing your lead-generation efforts.

Actionable Steps:

1. Profile Optimization:
    - Use ChatGPT to craft a compelling LinkedIn profile summary highlighting your expertise and value proposition.
    - Example Prompt: "Create a LinkedIn summary for a sales professional specializing in SaaS solutions."
2. Content Scheduling:
    - Develop a content calendar with the help of ChatGPT, ensuring regular and relevant posts.
    - Example Prompt: "Generate a monthly LinkedIn content calendar for a B2B sales manager."

3. Automated Engagement:

   - Set up ChatGPT to promptly respond to comments and messages, maintaining engagement without constant manual effort.
   - Example Prompt: "Draft responses to common LinkedIn comments about our new product launch."

Case Study:
XYZ Solutions implemented ChatGPT to manage their LinkedIn interactions. Within three months, they saw a 35% increase in post engagement and a 20% boost in lead conversions while reducing the time spent on manual engagement by 50%.

Develop Unique Content

Content creation can be a beast, but this is where ChatGPT truly shines. Need fresh ideas for blog posts? ChatGPT has got you covered. It's like having a brainstorming buddy who never lacks creative ideas. You can generate unique content that focuses on your audience's interests, keeping them engaged and returning for more.

Actionable Steps:

1. Topic Generation:
   - Use ChatGPT to brainstorm blog post ideas tailored to your audience's interests and industry trends.
   - Example Prompt: "Suggest ten blog topics for a company specializing in renewable energy solutions."
2. Content Drafting:
   - Draft initial blog posts with ChatGPT, then refine and personalize them to match your brand voice.
   - Example Prompt: "Write a 500-word blog post on the benefits of AI in sales automation."
3. SEO Optimization:
   - Incorporate SEO keywords suggested by ChatGPT to improve search engine rankings.
   - Example Prompt: "Optimize this blog post for SEO using the keywords: 'AI sales

automation,' 'lead generation tools,' and 'sales funnel optimization.'"

Potential Challenges & Solutions:

- Challenge: Ensuring content originality.
    - Solution: Use ChatGPT as a starting point and add unique insights or data to differentiate your content.

Case Study:

Content Creators Inc. leveraged ChatGPT to streamline its blog production. It increased its publishing frequency by 40% while maintaining high-quality standards, resulting in a 25% rise in organic traffic within four months.

Automate Social Media Engagement

Keeping up with social media can feel like trying to drink from a fire hose—overwhelming and impossible. But ChatGPT turns this chaos into a manageable stream. Social media is like a busy bazaar; you must be present to connect with your audience. ChatGPT helps by automating responses, managing customer queries, and ensuring your engagement doesn't fall into the abyss. Whether Twitter, Facebook, or LinkedIn, ChatGPT keeps your voice consistent across platforms.

Actionable Steps:

1. Automated Replies:
    - Set up ChatGPT to handle common queries and comments and provide timely responses.
    - Example Prompt: "Create automated replies for frequently asked questions about our product."
2. Content Repurposing:
    - Use ChatGPT to adapt blog content into social media posts tailored for each platform.
    - Example Prompt: "Transform this blog post into five engaging Twitter threads."
3. Engagement Tracking:
    - Monitor engagement metrics with ChatGPT's assistance to refine your social media strategy.

- Example Prompt: "Analyze our last month's social media engagement and suggest improvements."

Case Study:

ABC Marketing utilized ChatGPT to manage its social media accounts. Within six months, it achieved a 40% increase in follower engagement and a 25% rise in website traffic from social media channels.

Personalize and Automate Cold Emailing

No one likes receiving cold, impersonal emails. They're like junk mail for your inbox. But with ChatGPT, you can personalize hundreds of emails in no time. Imagine boosting your engagement rates with emails that feel like they were written just for the recipient. Follow-up responses? ChatGPT handles those, too, stepping up your email marketing game effortlessly.

Actionable Steps:

1. Email Templates:
   - Create personalized email templates with ChatGPT that can be easily customized for each lead.
   - Example Prompt: "Generate a personalized cold email template for reaching out to potential clients in the tech industry."
2. Automated Follow-ups:
   - Set up a sequence of follow-up emails that ChatGPT can send based on recipient interactions.
   - Example Prompt: "Draft three follow-up emails for leads who opened but did not respond to the initial email."
3. A/B Testing:
   - Use ChatGPT to generate different email variants for A/B testing to determine the most effective messages.
   - Example Prompt: "Create two versions of a cold email subject line to test which one has a higher open rate."

Potential Challenges & Solutions:

- Challenge: Avoiding spam filters.
    - Solution: Ensure emails are personalized and include valuable content, as suggested by ChatGPT, to improve deliverability.

Case Study:

SalesBoost Co. integrated ChatGPT into its email marketing strategy. It saw a 45% increase in open rates and a 30% boost in response rates, significantly enhancing its lead conversion pipeline.

Automate SEO-driven Lead Generation

SEO can be a tedious puzzle, but ChatGPT simplifies it. Need a keyword strategy? ChatGPT can whip one up in seconds. It's like having a personal SEO guru. With ChatGPT, you can optimize your content, generate more quality leads, and capture your audience's attention faster than ever.

Actionable Steps:

1. Keyword Research:
    - Use ChatGPT to identify high-impact keywords relevant to your industry and audience.
    - Example Prompt: "Provide a list of high-traffic keywords for a business offering online marketing services."
2. Content Optimization:
    - Optimize existing content with SEO best practices recommended by ChatGPT.
    - Example Prompt: "Improve the SEO of this article by incorporating the following keywords: 'digital marketing strategies,' 'SEO tips,' and 'lead generation.'"
3. Performance Monitoring:
    - Track SEO performance metrics with ChatGPT's assistance to adjust strategies as needed.
    - Example Prompt: "Analyze our website's SEO performance and suggest areas for improvement."

Case Study:

Tech Innovators integrated ChatGPT into their SEO strategy. Thanks to optimized content and effective keyword targeting, they experienced a 50% increase in organic traffic and a 30% rise in qualified leads within four months.

Customize Blog Content across Social Media Platforms

Each social media platform is like a different country regarding language and culture. What works on LinkedIn might flop on Twitter. ChatGPT helps you customize your content for each platform, ensuring it resonates with your audience. It's like having a multilingual translator who knows precisely what your audience wants.

Actionable Steps:

1. Platform-Specific Adaptation:
    - Tailor your blog content into platform-specific formats (e.g., infographics for Instagram, threads for Twitter) using ChatGPT.
    - Example Prompt: "Convert this blog post on sales automation into three engaging Instagram captions with relevant hashtags."
2. Consistent Branding:
    - Maintain a consistent brand voice across all platforms with the help of ChatGPT's guidance.
    - Example Prompt: "Ensure the following social media posts align with our brand voice: professional, friendly, and innovative."
3. Engagement Strategies:
    - Develop unique engagement strategies for each platform based on ChatGPT's insights.
    - Example Prompt: "Suggest engagement tactics for our Facebook page to increase community interaction."

Case Study:

Global Brands Ltd. utilized ChatGPT to customize their blog content for various social media platforms. This strategy led to a 60% increase in cross-platform engagement and a 35% improvement in content reach, enhancing their overall digital presence.

Closing More Deals with AI Help

Have you ever wondered how the best salespeople close deals? It's an art, and AI is the new brush. Sales reps use AI to improve communication and engagement with customers. In 2024, AI isn't just a tool; it's a game-changer. AI helps sales reps navigate the complex sales funnel, from lead generation to closing deals. By combining human intelligence with AI, sales pros create more opportunities and close deals.

Actionable Steps:

1. Lead Scoring:
   - Implement AI-driven lead scoring to prioritize high-potential leads using ChatGPT.
   - Example Prompt: "Develop a lead scoring system based on engagement metrics and demographic data."
2. Personalized Pitches:
   - Craft personalized sales pitches and proposals with ChatGPT's assistance to address specific client needs.
   - Example Prompt: "Create a personalized sales pitch for a potential client in the healthcare industry looking for CRM solutions."
3. Deal Tracking:
   - Use ChatGPT to monitor and track the progress of deals through the sales funnel, ensuring timely follow-ups.
   - Example Prompt: "Generate a weekly report on the status of all active deals and suggest next steps."

Relevant Example:

Take Amazon, for example. It uses AI to recommend products based on purchase history, set prices strategically, and outperform competitors. Sales reps can adopt similar AI tools to enhance their sales strategies and customer interactions.

Addressing Potential Challenges

While AI offers numerous benefits, integrating it into your sales funnels can be challenging. Here are some common obstacles and how to overcome them:

1. Data Privacy Concerns:
   - Solution: Ensure compliance with data protection regulations by using secure

AI tools and being transparent with customers about data usage.

    - Example Action: Implement GDPR-compliant AI solutions and communicate your data practices to clients.

2. Initial Setup Costs:
    - Solution: Start with affordable AI solutions and scale up as you see measurable benefits. Many AI tools offer tiered pricing based on usage.
    - Example Action: Begin with an essential ChatGPT subscription and expand functionalities as ROI becomes evident.
3. Learning Curve:
    - Solution: Train your team to utilize AI tools like ChatGPT effectively. Provide resources and support to ease the transition.
    - Example Action: Organize workshops and provide access to online tutorials so your sales team can proficiently use ChatGPT.
4. Maintaining Human Touch:
    - Solution: Use AI to handle repetitive tasks, allowing your sales team to focus on building genuine relationships with clients.
    - Example Action: Automate routine follow-ups with ChatGPT while dedicating more time to personalized client interactions.
5. Integration with Existing Systems:
    - Solution: Choose AI tools that seamlessly integrate with your current CRM and sales platforms to ensure smooth workflows.
    - Example Action: Select ChatGPT-compatible CRM systems and utilize APIs for seamless data flow.

Reflection Prompt:

Consider a recent content project you worked on. How could AI have improved your process? Reflect on balancing AI assistance and your creative input to enhance efficiency and quality.

Additional Resources:

- AI Integration Tools: Zapier, HubSpot, Salesforce Einstein

- NLP Learning Platforms: Coursera NLP Courses, edX NLP Programs
- Community Forums: Engage with other users on platforms like Reddit's r/OpenAI and LinkedIn Groups
- Ethical AI Guidelines: OpenAI's Responsible AI Practices

Chapter 9: Strategy 7 – Financial Forecasting and Analysis

Leveraging AI for Data-Driven Decision-Making

Imagine you're running a mid-sized company, constantly juggling financial data, trying to make sense of it all. It's a daunting task, filled with spreadsheets and endless numbers. Then, you discover AI, and suddenly, financial decision-making feels like a breeze. AI is like having a financial wizard who can contextualize complex data in seconds—minus the pointy hat and magical robes.

1. Automating Financial Analysis

Streamlining Financial Processes with ChatGPT

Forget those sci-fi movies where AI is a robot taking over the world. AI is your trusty sidekick, helping you navigate uncertain financial waters. Many companies now use AI to streamline, analyze, and forecast their financial data, making them more adaptable to market fluctuations.

Benefits:

- Efficiency: Automates repetitive financial tasks, saving time and reducing errors.
- Accuracy: Enhances data accuracy by minimizing human error in data entry and analysis.
- Scalability: Easily scales with your business growth, handling increasing volumes of data effortlessly.

Example:

Prompt: "Analyze the last quarter's sales data and identify key trends."

ChatGPT Response: "Based on the last quarter's sales data, there was a 15% increase in online sales compared to the previous quarter, primarily driven by a successful digital marketing campaign. Additionally, sales in the European market grew by 20%, while the North American market saw a 10% decline due to increased competition."

Case Study: FinTech Solutions

- Challenge: High volume of financial data with manual analysis leading to delays.
- Solution: Integrated ChatGPT to automate data analysis and reporting.
- Results: Reduced analysis time by 50%, improved accuracy, and enabled real-time financial insights.

Action Step:

Implement ChatGPT to automate your financial data analysis, generate real-time reports, and identify key trends to inform strategic decisions.

Reflection Prompt:

How can automating your financial analysis with ChatGPT improve your decision-making process and operational efficiency?

Implementation Guide:

1. Data Integration:
    - Connect your financial databases (e.g., ERP systems) with ChatGPT using APIs.
2. Template Creation:
    - Develop standard prompts and templates for regular financial reports.
3. Automation Setup:
    - Schedule automated queries and report generation at desired intervals.
4. Review and Iterate:
    - Regularly review AI-generated reports for accuracy and make necessary adjustments to prompts.

Technical Insights:

ChatGPT processes financial data by leveraging Natural Language Processing (NLP) to interpret and analyze numerical and categorical data. It identifies patterns, trends, and anomalies by comparing current data against historical datasets, enabling accurate and timely financial analysis.

2. Enhancing Predictability with AI

Moving Beyond Conventional Forecasting Methods

AI helps companies move past traditional financial forecasting methods. Instead of relying solely on historical data, AI can analyze many variables to predict future trends. This makes your company agile and ready to tackle economic or market conditions. Imagine AI as your financial weather forecaster, predicting sunny days and stormy weather ahead—without the need for an umbrella.

Benefits:

- Advanced Predictions: Utilizes multiple data sources for more accurate forecasting.
- Risk Management: Identifies potential financial risks early, allowing for proactive measures.
- Agility: Enables swift adjustments to financial strategies based on predictive insights.

Example:

Prompt: "Forecast the next quarter's revenue based on current market trends and historical data."

ChatGPT Response: "Considering the current market trends and historical sales data, the next quarter's revenue is projected to increase by 10%. This growth is expected to be driven by a 20% rise in product X sales and a 15% increase in service Y subscriptions."

Case Study: Retail Innovators Inc.

- Challenge: Inaccurate revenue forecasts affecting inventory management.
- Solution: Utilized ChatGPT for comprehensive financial forecasting incorporating market trends and internal data.
- Results: Achieved a 25% improvement in forecast accuracy, leading to better inventory management and reduced costs.

Action Step:

Use ChatGPT to enhance your revenue forecasting by integrating various data points, including market trends, sales data, and economic indicators.

Reflection Prompt:

How can enhancing your financial predictability with AI-driven forecasting improve your business's adaptability and strategic planning?

Implementation Guide:

1. Data Aggregation:

- Collect data from diverse sources such as sales records, market reports, and economic indicators.

2. Model Training:

   - Train ChatGPT with historical data to recognize patterns and correlations.

3. Scenario Analysis:

   - Use AI to simulate different market scenarios and their potential impact on revenue.

4. Continuous Monitoring:

   - Regularly update the model with new data to refine predictions.

Technical Insights:
ChatGPT employs machine learning algorithms to analyze vast datasets, identifying correlations between financial indicators and market conditions. It continuously updates its forecasting models by incorporating real-time data, ensuring predictions remain accurate and relevant.

3. Customizing Financial Models

Tailored Financial Forecasting for Unique Business Needs
Every company is unique, and so should its financial forecasting approach. AI allows businesses to personalize their analysis, considering internal and external factors. Think of AI as a tailor, customizing a suit that fits your company perfectly rather than a one-size-fits-all solution.

Benefits:

- Customization: Adapts financial models to specific business needs and industry nuances.
- Comprehensive Analysis: Incorporates various factors, including market conditions, competitor performance, and internal operations.
- Enhanced Accuracy: Provides more precise forecasts by accounting for unique business variables.

Example:

Prompt: "Create a customized financial model for a SaaS company considering user growth, subscription rates, and churn."

ChatGPT Response: "Based on the inputs, the financial model projects a user growth rate of 15% monthly, an average subscription rate of $50 per user, and a churn rate of 5% per month. The projected monthly revenue will grow as follows:

- Month 1: 1,000 users * $50 = $50,000
- Month 2: (1,000 * 1.15) * $50 - (1,000 * 0.05) * $50 = $57,500
- Month 3: (1,150 * 1.15) * $50 - (1,150 * 0.05) * $50 = $66,125
- ... and so on."

Case Study: TechStart Ventures

- Challenge: Generic financial models must reflect their tech products' unique aspects.
- Solution: Customized financial models using ChatGPT to incorporate specific growth metrics and market dynamics.
- Results: Improved financial planning accuracy by 30%, leading to better investment decisions and resource allocation.

Action Step:

Develop customized financial models with ChatGPT by inputting your unique business variables and forecasting requirements.

Reflection Prompt:

How can customizing your financial models with AI ensure more accurate and relevant financial forecasts for your business?

Implementation Guide:

1. Define Unique Variables:
   - Identify critical factors specific to your business, such as user acquisition rates, subscription tiers, and churn rates.
2. Model Design:
   - Create prompts that incorporate these variables to generate tailored financial projections.
3. Integration:

- Link ChatGPT with your CRM and sales platforms to automatically update variables based on real-time data.

4. Validation:

   - Regularly compare AI-generated forecasts with actual performance to ensure accuracy and adjust as needed.

Technical Insights:
ChatGPT can be fine-tuned with industry-specific data to enhance the relevance and accuracy of financial models. By integrating with your existing business systems, it can pull real-time data to continuously update and refine forecasts, ensuring they remain aligned with your business dynamics.

4. Maximizing Profitability and Growth

Strategic Decision-Making with AI Insights
Before a business becomes profitable, it must navigate through a series of strategic decisions. AI allows companies to maximize profit margins by streamlining tasks that otherwise take up valuable time. It's like having an efficiency expert who ensures everything runs smoothly. And just like that one friend who always finds the best deals, AI helps you cut costs and save big.

Benefits:

- Cost Reduction: Identifies areas where costs can be minimized without compromising quality.
- Profit Optimization: Highlights opportunities to increase profit margins through strategic adjustments.
- Resource Allocation: Ensures resources are allocated efficiently to maximize returns.

Example:
Prompt: "Identify cost-saving opportunities in our current operational expenses."
ChatGPT Response: "Based on your operational expenses, consider the following cost-saving opportunities:

1. Supplier Negotiations: Renegotiate contracts with suppliers to secure better rates.
2. Energy Efficiency: Invest in energy-efficient equipment to reduce utility bills.

3. Automate Routine Tasks: Implement automation for repetitive tasks to reduce labor costs.

4. Optimize Inventory Levels: Adjust inventory levels to prevent overstocking and reduce storage costs."

Case Study: GrowthMakers LLC

- Challenge: High operational costs affecting profitability.
- Solution: Utilized ChatGPT to analyze expenses and identify cost-saving measures.
- Results: Achieved a 20% reduction in operational costs and a 15% increase in profit margins within six months.

Action Step:

Leverage ChatGPT to analyze your operational expenses and identify strategic cost-saving opportunities to enhance profitability.

Reflection Prompt:

How can maximizing your profitability with AI-driven cost analysis and optimization strategies impact your business growth?

Implementation Guide:

1. Expense Data Collection:
   - Gather detailed data on all operational expenses across departments.
2. Cost Analysis Prompts:
   - Use ChatGPT to analyze each expense category and identify potential savings.
3. Implement Recommendations:
   - Act on the identified cost-saving measures, such as renegotiating contracts or automating tasks.
4. Monitor and Adjust:
   - Continuously monitor the impact of implemented changes and adjust strategies as necessary.

Technical Insights:

ChatGPT can perform a granular analysis of your expense data by categorizing costs, identifying patterns of overspending, and suggesting targeted cost-saving measures. Integrating with your financial software can provide real-time insights and recommendations, ensuring ongoing optimization of your profitability strategies.

5. Sales and Growth Prediction

Accurate Forecasting for Strategic Growth

With AI, sales reps can now predict their yearly or quarterly sales accurately. Instead of the old-school method of guessing costs, AI predictive analytics can forecast extensive data without errors. This allows business heads to review real-time data and make informed decisions that drive growth. Imagine having a crystal ball that shows you exactly how many products you'll sell next quarter without the mystical fog and eerie music.

Benefits:

- Precision: Provides accurate sales forecasts based on comprehensive data analysis.
- Strategic Planning: Enables informed decision-making for inventory management, marketing strategies, and resource allocation.
- Risk Mitigation: Identifies potential sales dips early, allowing for proactive measures.

Example:

Prompt: "Predict our next quarter's sales based on current trends and historical data."

ChatGPT Response: "Considering the current sales trends and historical data, the next quarter's sales are projected to increase by 12%. The upcoming product launch and a targeted marketing campaign primarily drive this growth. Additionally, seasonal factors are expected to contribute an additional 5% increase in sales."

Case Study: RetailForward Inc.

- Challenge: Inaccurate sales predictions leading to overstocking and stockouts.
- Solution: Implemented ChatGPT for sales and growth prediction.
- Results: Improved sales forecast accuracy by 25%, leading to better inventory management and increased sales by 18%.

Action Step:

Use ChatGPT to generate accurate sales forecasts, enabling better strategic planning and resource allocation to drive business growth.

Reflection Prompt:

How can accurate sales and growth predictions with ChatGPT enhance your strategic planning and overall business performance?

Implementation Guide:

1. Historical Data Input:
    - Provide ChatGPT with comprehensive historical sales data.
2. Trend Analysis:
    - Use AI to identify underlying sales trends and patterns.
3. Forecast Generation:
    - Generate sales forecasts based on current trends, upcoming promotions, and market conditions.
4. Integration with CRM:
    - Integrate forecasts with your CRM system to align sales strategies with predictions.
5. Continuous Refinement:
    - Update the model regularly with new sales data to improve forecast accuracy.

Technical Insights:

ChatGPT leverages time-series analysis and machine-learning algorithms to interpret historical sales data and market trends. It refines its forecasting models by continuously learning from new data inputs, ensuring sales predictions remain accurate and relevant to changing business dynamics.

6. Predictive Maintenance

Preventing Operational Disruptions with AI

Predictive maintenance is essential to AI, allowing businesses to foresee and resolve issues before they disrupt operations. Think of it as having an intelligent assistant who reminds you to service your equipment before it breaks down, saving you time and money. It's like your car sending you a friendly nudge reminder before it decides to quit on you during a road trip.

Benefits:

- Downtime Reduction: Minimizes unexpected equipment failures and operational interruptions.
- Cost Savings: Prevents costly repairs by addressing issues proactively.
- Extended Equipment Lifespan: Maintains machinery optimally, prolonging its useful life.

Example:

Prompt: "Identify potential maintenance issues in our production line based on usage data."

ChatGPT Response: "Based on the current usage data, the following potential maintenance issues have been identified:

1. Conveyor Belt Wear: High usage indicates potential wear and tear; recommend inspection and possible replacement within the next month.
2. Motor Overheating: Increased temperature readings suggest possible motor inefficiency; servicing is recommended to prevent failure.
3. Hydraulic System Leaks: Detection of fluid loss in the hydraulic system; recommend immediate inspection and repair to avoid operational disruptions."

Case Study: ManufacturingPros Ltd.

- Challenge: Frequent equipment breakdowns causing production delays.
- Solution: Utilized ChatGPT for predictive maintenance analysis.
- Results: Reduced equipment downtime by 30% and maintenance costs by 20% through proactive issue resolution.

Action Step:

Implement ChatGPT to analyze equipment usage data and predict maintenance needs, ensuring smooth and uninterrupted operations.

Reflection Prompt:

How can predictive maintenance with ChatGPT help you prevent operational disruptions and reduce maintenance costs?

Implementation Guide:

1. Data Collection:
    - Gather real-time usage data from all machinery and equipment.
2. Condition Monitoring:
    - Use ChatGPT to monitor equipment conditions and identify signs of wear or potential failure.
3. Maintenance Scheduling:
    - Schedule maintenance activities based on AI predictions to prevent unexpected breakdowns.
4. Feedback Loop:
    - Continuously feed maintenance outcomes back into ChatGPT to improve prediction accuracy.

Technical Insights:

ChatGPT analyzes sensor data and usage patterns to predict equipment failures before they occur. By integrating with IoT devices and machinery sensors, it can monitor real-time data, identify anomalies, and trigger maintenance alerts. This proactive approach ensures equipment remains in optimal condition, reducing the likelihood of unexpected downtime.

7. Inventory Management

Optimizing Stock Levels with AI Precision

Successful companies understand the importance of flawless inventory management. Take Toyota, for instance. It uses AI models to streamline its inventory across different countries. AI helps bridge the gap between supply and demand, ensuring companies stock just the right amount of products. It's like having a perfect balance scale that always gets it right, ensuring you're not left with too many or too few products.

Benefits:

- Demand Forecasting: Accurately predicts product demand to optimize stock levels.
- Cost Reduction: Minimizes holding costs and reduces the risk of overstocking or stockouts.
- Efficiency: Streamlines inventory processes, improving overall operational efficiency.

Example:

Prompt: "Optimize our inventory levels for the upcoming holiday season based on past sales data and current trends."

ChatGPT Response: "Based on past holiday sales data and current market trends, it is recommended to increase inventory levels for the following products:

1. Product A: Increase stock by 20% due to a rising trend in customer demand.
2. Product B: Maintain current levels as demand remains stable.
3. Product C: Decrease stock by 10% to avoid overstocking based on predicted lower sales. Additionally, implement just-in-time inventory practices to optimize stock levels further and reduce holding costs."

Case Study: HomeStyle Furnishings

- Challenge: Inaccurate inventory forecasting leads to overstocking of low-demand items.
- Solution: Integrated ChatGPT for inventory management and demand forecasting.
- Results: Achieved a 25% reduction in holding costs and a 15% increase in inventory turnover rate.

Action Step:

Use ChatGPT to analyze your sales data and current market trends, optimize your inventory levels, and ensure you have the right products in the right quantities.

Reflection Prompt:

How can optimizing your inventory management with ChatGPT improve your operational efficiency and reduce costs?

Implementation Guide:

1. Sales Data Analysis:
   - Input historical sales data into ChatGPT to identify demand patterns.
2. Trend Identification:
   - Use AI to detect emerging market trends and seasonal variations.
3. Stock Level Adjustment:
   - Adjust inventory levels based on AI recommendations to prevent overstocking or stockouts.

4. Just-In-Time Implementation:

    - Integrate ChatGPT with your supply chain to adopt just-in-time inventory practices, reducing holding costs.

Technical Insights:
ChatGPT utilizes predictive analytics to forecast demand based on historical sales data, market trends, and external factors such as economic indicators. Integrating with inventory management systems can provide real-time recommendations on stock levels, ensuring optimal inventory turnover and minimizing holding costs.

Conclusion: Harnessing the Power of AI for Financial Forecasting and Analysis

By embracing AI tools like ChatGPT, leveraging data for insights, customizing financial models, maximizing profitability, and prioritizing continuous learning, you can unlock AI's full potential for economic forecasting and analysis. Embrace innovation, experiment boldly, and stay agile to thrive in the dynamic world of business finance.

Key Takeaways:

- AI is a Tool, Not a Replacement: Combine AI capabilities with human expertise to make informed financial decisions.
- Quality Over Quantity: Focus on accurate and insightful financial data analysis to drive strategic growth.
- Ethics Matter: Uphold transparency, integrity, and fairness in all AI-assisted financial processes.
- Strategic Integration: Implement ChatGPT thoughtfully to maximize benefits and ensure seamless integration with existing systems.
- Continuous Learning: Stay updated with AI advancements and refine your financial strategies.

Action Steps:

1. Implement AI Tools:

    - Start using ChatGPT for financial data analysis, forecasting, and reporting to streamline your financial workflows.

2. Optimize for Accuracy:

- Utilize ChatGPT to enhance your financial models with accurate predictions and insights.

3. Monetize Thoughtfully:

    - Explore and integrate monetization strategies that align with your financial goals and business needs.

4. Maintain Ethical Standards:

    - Establish guidelines to ensure your AI-assisted financial processes remain accurate, unbiased, and transparent.

5. Continuous Learning:

    - Stay updated with the latest AI advancements in financial technology and continuously refine your forecasting strategies to stay competitive.

Reflection Prompt:

Consider a recent financial project you worked on. How could AI have improved your process? Reflect on the balance between AI assistance and human expertise.

Chapter 10: Strategy 8 - Efficient Talent Acquisition

Streamlining the Recruitment Process with AI

Imagine this: You're an HR professional buried under a mountain of resumes, trying to find the perfect candidate for a critical role. It's overwhelming, right? Enter AI, your new best friend in recruitment. AI is like having a personal assistant who never sleeps, tirelessly sorting through resumes, scheduling interviews, and engaging candidates without needing a coffee break.

1. Automating the Recruitment Process

Revolutionizing Recruitment with AI

For years, streamlining has been a tried-and-true approach to increasing hiring efficiency. AI has been around for a while, but it's fascinating to see how HR professionals are now fully embracing it. AI recruiting tools have transformed the way businesses recruit and retain top talent. They handle time-consuming, repetitive tasks, allowing recruiters to focus on more strategic activities—like finding that unicorn candidate or, you know, actually taking a lunch break.

Benefits:

- Efficiency: Automates repetitive tasks, saving time and resources.
- Precision: Enhances the accuracy of candidate screening and matching.
- Scalability: Easily scales with your hiring needs, whether you're recruiting for one position or a hundred.

Example:

Prompt: "Automate the initial screening of resumes for a software developer position."

ChatGPT Response: "Based on the provided resumes, the following candidates meet the criteria for a software developer position:

1. Jane Doe: 5 years of experience in Python and Java, excellent problem-solving skills.

2. John Smith: 3 years of experience in JavaScript and React, a strong portfolio of projects.

3. Emily Davis: 4 years of experience in C++ and machine learning, proactive team player. Candidates not meeting the essential criteria have been flagged for further review if necessary."

Case Study: TalentBoost Inc.

- Challenge: Overwhelmed by the volume of applications for multiple job openings.
- Solution: Implemented an AI-powered recruitment tool to automate resume screening and initial candidate outreach.
- Results: Reduced time-to-hire by 40%, increased candidate satisfaction, and improved overall hiring quality.

Action Step:

Integrate an AI recruitment tool into your hiring process to automate resume screening and initial candidate outreach, freeing up your time to engage with top talent.

Reflection Prompt:

How can automating your recruitment process with AI tools enhance your hiring efficiency and allow you to focus on strategic HR initiatives?

Implementation Guide:

1. Choose the Right AI Tool:
    - Research and select an AI-powered recruitment platform that aligns with your hiring needs.
2. Integrate with Existing Systems:
    - Connect the AI tool with your Applicant Tracking System (ATS) for seamless data flow.
3. Define Screening Criteria:
    - Set up specific criteria for automated resume screening based on job requirements.

4. Train the AI:

    - Input historical hiring data to train the AI for better accuracy in candidate matching.

5. Monitor and Adjust:

    - Regularly review AI performance and adjust parameters to improve screening accuracy.

Technical Insights:
AI recruitment tools utilize machine learning algorithms and natural language processing (NLP) to analyze and interpret resume data. By learning from historical hiring patterns and job requirements, these tools can effectively identify the most suitable candidates, reducing the burden of manual screening and enhancing the overall recruitment process.

2. Hit Perfect Matches

Finding the Ideal Candidate Made Easy
Finding the ideal candidate can be like searching for a needle in a haystack. AI streamlines this process by assessing criteria and finding candidates with similar interests and characteristics. It's like having a matchmaking service for job seekers and employers—minus the awkward first dates.

Benefits:

- Enhanced Matching: Utilizes advanced algorithms to match candidates with job requirements accurately.
- Reduced Time-to-Fill: Speeds up the hiring process by quickly identifying top candidates.
- Improved Candidate Quality: Ensures a better fit between the candidate's skills and the job role.

Example:
Prompt: "Find candidates with experience in project management and proficiency in Agile methodologies."
ChatGPT Response: "Based on the current applicant pool, the following candidates match the criteria:

1. Michael Brown: 6 years of project management experience, certified Scrum Master.

2. Sarah Lee: 4 years of experience in Agile project management, adept at leading cross-functional teams.

3. David Wilson: 5 years managing Agile projects in the tech industry, excellent stakeholder communication skills."

Case Study: HireSmart LLC

- Challenge: Difficulty in identifying candidates with specific project management skills.

- Solution: Deployed an AI tool to filter candidates based on project management experience and Agile proficiency.

- Results: Increased the quality of hires by 35%, shortened the hiring cycle by 25%, and enhanced team productivity.

Action Step:

Use an AI recruitment tool to filter candidates based on specific skills and experience, ensuring a higher quality of hires that align with your organizational needs.

Reflection Prompt:

How can AI-driven candidate matching improve the quality of your hires and reduce the time spent on the recruitment process?

Implementation Guide:

1. Define Key Skills and Experience:
    - Clearly outline the essential skills and experiences required for the role.

2. Customize Matching Criteria:
    - Input these criteria into the AI tool to tailor the candidate-matching process.

3. Review Matched Candidates:
    - Examine the list of matched candidates and shortlist for interviews.

4. Continuous Learning:
    - Provide feedback to the AI tool to refine and improve future candidate matching accuracy.

Technical Insights:

AI-driven candidate matching leverages data from resumes, job descriptions, and performance metrics to assess compatibility. By analyzing factors such as skills, experience, education, and even cultural fit indicators, AI ensures that the most suitable candidates are highlighted for each position.

3. Avoid Bias and Discrimination

Creating a Fair and Inclusive Recruitment Process

AI can help create a fairer recruitment process by ensuring no applicant is unfairly evaluated based on race, gender, or other biases. It promotes inclusivity and diversity, making the hiring process more objective and transparent—turning the hiring hall into a merit-based arena.

Benefits:

- Objective Screening: Reduces unconscious bias by focusing solely on candidate qualifications.
- Enhanced Diversity: Promotes a more diverse and inclusive workforce.
- Legal Compliance: Helps ensure compliance with equal employment opportunity laws.

Example:

Prompt: "Evaluate candidates for a marketing position based solely on their skills and experience, excluding personal demographics."

ChatGPT Response: "After excluding personal demographic information, the following candidates are recommended based on their skills and experience:

1. Linda Martinez: 5 years in digital marketing, expertise in SEO and content strategy.
2. James Thompson: 4 years of experience in social media marketing, strong analytical skills.
3. Karen White: 6 years in brand management, proficient in market research and campaign planning."

Case Study: DiverseHire Inc.

- Challenge: Unconscious bias in the recruitment process affecting diversity.
- Solution: Implemented an AI-based recruitment tool that anonymizes resumes and

focuses on skills and experience.

- Results: Increased workforce diversity by 20%, improved employee satisfaction, and enhanced company reputation.

Action Step:
Adopt an AI recruitment tool that anonymizes candidate information and focuses on objective criteria to promote a fair and unbiased hiring process.

Reflection Prompt:
In what ways can AI-assisted unbiased recruitment practices enhance your organization's diversity and inclusion efforts?

Implementation Guide:

1. Select Bias-Free AI Tools:
   - Choose AI recruitment platforms that are designed to minimize bias.
2. Anonymize Candidate Data:
   - Ensure the AI tool removes personal demographic information from resumes.
3. Focus on Objective Criteria:
   - Set up the AI to evaluate candidates based on skills, experience, and qualifications.
4. Monitor Outcomes:
   - Regularly review hiring outcomes to ensure diversity goals are met and adjust AI parameters if necessary.

Technical Insights:
AI recruitment tools can be programmed to disregard personal demographic information and focus solely on objective data such as skills, experience, and qualifications. By analyzing candidates based on standardized criteria, AI helps eliminate unconscious biases often influencing human recruiters, fostering a more equitable hiring process.

4. AI-Based Talent Acquisition: Key Innovations

Harnessing Cutting-Edge AI Technologies for Recruitment

AI sourcing solutions can automate recruitment, from screening resumes to engaging candidates with AI-powered chatbots. These tools provide real-time candidate participation, making the process more efficient and engaging. Natural Language Processing (NLP) solutions help extract and clarify information during recruitment, streamlining operations and turning your recruitment strategy into a high-tech powerhouse.

Benefits:

- Comprehensive Automation: Streamlines every step of the recruitment process.
- Enhanced Candidate Engagement: Keeps candidates informed and engaged throughout the hiring journey.
- Data-Driven Insights: Provides actionable insights to refine recruitment strategies.

Example:

Prompt: "Use AI to automate candidate outreach for a sales manager position."

ChatGPT Response: "Initiating automated outreach for the sales manager position:

1. Initial Contact: Send personalized emails to shortlisted candidates introducing the role.
2. Follow-Up Messages: Scheduling follow-up emails and messages to engage interested candidates.
3. Interview Scheduling: Automating the scheduling of interviews based on candidate availability.
4. Feedback Collection: Gathering feedback from candidates post-interview to improve the recruitment process."

Case Study: TalentWave LLC

- Challenge: Low candidate engagement and high drop-off rates during the recruitment process.
- Solution: Deployed AI-powered chatbots to engage candidates, answer queries, and schedule interviews.
- Results: Increased candidate engagement by 40%, reduced drop-off rates by 30%, and accelerated the hiring timeline.

Action Step:

Implement AI-powered chatbots in your recruitment process to enhance candidate engagement, answer queries, and streamline interview scheduling.

Reflection Prompt:
How can AI-based talent acquisition innovations improve candidate engagement and streamline your recruitment operations?

Implementation Guide:

1. Integrate AI Chatbots:
   - Deploy AI chatbots to interact with candidates on your careers page and recruitment platforms.
2. Automate Communication:
   - Set up automated responses for familiar candidate inquiries and follow-up messages.
3. Schedule Interviews:
   - Use AI to coordinate interview schedules based on mutual availability.
4. Analyze Engagement Metrics:
   - Monitor chatbot interactions to identify areas for improving candidate engagement.

Technical Insights:
AI-powered chatbots utilize Natural Language Processing (NLP) to understand and respond to candidate inquiries in real-time. By automating communication and scheduling, these chatbots ensure a seamless and engaging candidate experience while providing valuable data on candidate interactions to inform and enhance recruitment strategies.

5. Optimize Recruitment Process

Enhancing Efficiency and Effectiveness with AI
AI is transforming the recruiting industry by improving the entire hiring process. It helps recruiters close gaps, optimize the recruitment process, and find the best candidates faster. Think of AI as your recruitment GPS, guiding you through the hiring journey with precision and efficiency.

Benefits:

- Process Optimization: Streamlines recruitment workflows for maximum efficiency.
- Enhanced Decision-Making: Provides data-driven insights to inform hiring decisions.
- Faster Hiring: Reduces time-to-fill positions by automating key recruitment steps.

Example:

Prompt: "Optimize the recruitment process for a remote marketing coordinator role using AI."

ChatGPT Response: "Optimizing the recruitment process for a remote marketing coordinator role:

1. Job Posting Automation: Use AI to simultaneously distribute the job posting across multiple platforms.
2. Resume Screening: Implement AI to filter resumes based on predefined criteria.
3. Candidate Engagement: Deploy AI chatbots to interact with candidates, answer questions, and schedule interviews.
4. Interview Assessment: Utilize AI tools to analyze interview responses and provide objective evaluations.
5. Offer Management: Automate the offer letter generation and approval process with AI assistance."

Case Study: RecruitRight Inc.

- Challenge: Inefficient recruitment workflows cause delays in filling key positions.
- Solution: Implemented AI-driven process optimization tools to streamline recruitment workflows.
- Results: Decreased time-to-fill by 35%, improved hiring accuracy, and enhanced overall recruitment efficiency.

Action Step:

Use AI-driven tools to optimize your recruitment workflows, ensuring a faster and more efficient hiring process that delivers high-quality candidates.

Reflection Prompt:

How can optimizing your recruitment process with AI enhance your hiring speed and accuracy?

Implementation Guide:

1. Map Current Recruitment Processes:
    - Identify and document existing recruitment workflows.
2. Identify Bottlenecks:
    - Use AI analytics to pinpoint inefficiencies and delays in the process.
3. Implement AI Solutions:
    - Deploy AI tools to automate and streamline identified bottlenecks.
4. Monitor and Refine:
    - Continuously monitor the optimized processes and make adjustments as needed for ongoing improvement.

Technical Insights:

AI process optimization tools analyze recruitment workflows to identify inefficiencies and suggest improvements. By automating repetitive tasks and providing actionable insights, these tools enhance the hiring process's speed and quality, ensuring that recruiters can focus on strategic initiatives and candidate engagement.

6. Connect and Engage with Potential Applicants

Enhancing Candidate Communication with AI

Candidate engagement is a constant process. AI messaging tools can revolutionize how recruiters communicate with applicants, making the process faster and more efficient. It's like having a personal assistant who can quickly find the right candidate, narrowing your search by geography, industry, age, and job title—without endless coffee runs.

Benefits:

- Consistent Communication: Ensures timely and consistent interactions with candidates.
- Personalized Engagement: Tailors send messages to individual candidates based on their profiles and preferences.
- Enhanced Candidate Experience: Improves the overall experience for candidates, increasing their interest and engagement.

Example:

Prompt: "Use AI to engage with candidates who applied for the graphic designer position."

ChatGPT Response: "Initiating engagement for graphic designer applicants:

1. Initial Outreach: Send personalized welcome emails to all applicants to thank them for their interest.

2. Follow-Up Messages: Dispatching follow-up messages to check their continued interest and availability.

3. Interview Invitations: Automatically schedule interviews for shortlisted candidates based on their availability.

4. Feedback Requests: Sending post-interview feedback requests to all candidates to improve the recruitment process."

Case Study: CreativeHire Ltd.

- Challenge: Low engagement rates with candidates lead to high drop-off during recruitment.

- Solution: Implemented AI messaging tools to automate and personalize candidate communications.

- Results: Increased candidate engagement by 50%, reduced drop-off rates by 20%, and improved overall candidate satisfaction.

Action Step:

Deploy AI messaging tools to automate and personalize your candidate communications, ensuring timely and engaging interactions that keep candidates interested throughout the recruitment process.

Reflection Prompt:

How can AI-driven candidate engagement tools improve your communication efficiency and enhance the overall candidate experience?

Implementation Guide:

1. Set Up Automated Messaging:

    - Configure AI tools to send automated messages at critical stages of the recruitment process.

2. Personalize Communications:

    - Use candidate data to tailor messages and make interactions more personalized.

3. Schedule Timely Follow-Ups:

    - Ensure that follow-up messages are sent promptly to maintain candidate interest.

4. Analyze Engagement Metrics:

    - Monitor response rates and engagement levels to refine your communication strategies.

Technical Insights:

AI messaging tools utilize machine learning and NLP to craft and send personalized communications to candidates. By analyzing candidate data and interaction history, these tools ensure that messages are relevant, timely, and engaging, enhancing the overall candidate experience and increasing the likelihood of successful hires.

Conclusion: Embracing AI for Efficient Talent Acquisition

AI in recruitment is no longer a futuristic dream—it's a game-changer happening right now. Imagine shaving hours off your hiring process, finding perfect candidates effortlessly, and building a diverse, talented team without bias. That's the power of AI. With AI tools, you can automate repetitive tasks, streamline candidate screening, and enhance engagement. It's like having a super-smart assistant who's always on the job, ensuring you never miss out on top talent.

So, why not harness this technology? Dive into the AI-driven future of recruitment. It's efficient, fair, and incredibly effective. Embrace AI and watch your talent acquisition process transform, making hiring more accessible and innovative.

Chapter 11: Strategy 9 – AI-Enhanced Product Development

Accelerating Innovation with ChatGPT

Imagine you're a product manager striving to outpace the competition. The development process feels sluggish, ideas become repetitive, and innovation seems out of reach. Then, you integrate AI—specifically ChatGPT—into your workflow, and everything changes. Product development becomes faster, more efficient, and brimming with creative possibilities. It's like having a tireless genius collaborator who always has fresh ideas, minus the eccentricities.

1. Automating the Product Development Process

Revolutionizing Development with AI

Traditional product development often involves repetitive tasks that consume valuable time and resources. ChatGPT can automate these tasks, allowing product managers and developers to focus on innovation and strategic thinking. You can accelerate development cycles, reduce errors, and enhance precision by leveraging AI.

Benefits:

- Efficiency: Automates routine tasks, freeing up time for creative problem-solving.
- Precision: Minimizes human error, enhancing the accuracy of development processes.
- Scalability: Handles multiple projects simultaneously, scaling with your product portfolio.

Example:

Suppose you're a product manager at a software company developing a new mobile application. You can use ChatGPT to automate the drafting of product specifications.

Prompt: "Draft initial product specifications for a mobile app that helps users track their carbon footprint."

ChatGPT Response:

- Features:
    - Track daily activities (transportation, energy use, diet) to calculate carbon emissions.
    - Provide tips to reduce carbon footprint based on user data.
    - Social sharing to encourage community challenges.
- User Interface:
    - Intuitive dashboard with visual graphs.
    - Customizable alerts and notifications.
- Technical Requirements:
    - Integration with GPS and health data.
    - Secure data storage and privacy compliance.

Technical Insights:

ChatGPT uses Natural Language Processing (NLP) and machine learning algorithms trained on vast datasets, including product specifications and industry standards. By understanding context and requirements, ChatGPT generates detailed and coherent specifications that align with your project's objectives.

Case Study: EcoTrack Innovations

- Challenge: Lengthy specification phases delaying product launches.
- Solution: Implemented ChatGPT to automate the initial drafting of product specs.
- Results: Reduced drafting time by 50%, accelerated development cycles, and launched the app two months ahead of schedule.

Action Step:

Integrate ChatGPT into your product development workflow to automate the creation of initial product specifications. This will allow your team to concentrate on refining and innovating.

Reflection Prompt:

How can automating the initial stages of product development with ChatGPT streamline your workflow and enhance your team's focus on innovation?

2. Speeding Up Innovation

Launching New Products Quickly with AI

Time-to-market is critical in today's fast-paced environment. ChatGPT can help you swiftly generate compelling marketing and advertising content, ensuring your product reaches the audience effectively.

Benefits:

- Rapid Content Generation: Produces high-quality marketing materials quickly.
- Consistency: Maintains a uniform brand voice across various platforms.
- Flexibility: Adapts content for different marketing channels and formats.

Example:

A marketing manager at a sustainable fashion brand needs to launch a new eco-friendly clothing line. Using ChatGPT, they generate engaging product descriptions and social media posts.

Prompt: "Create a catchy product description for a new line of sustainable denim jeans."

ChatGPT Response:

"Introducing our EcoDenim Collection—the perfect blend of style and sustainability. Crafted from 100% organic cotton and recycled materials, these jeans offer comfort without compromising the planet. Join us in making a fashion statement that matters."

Technical Insights:

ChatGPT's language generation capabilities stem from its training on diverse textual data, enabling it to produce creative and persuasive marketing content that resonates with target audiences.

Case Study: GreenThreads Apparel

- Challenge: Limited marketing resources causing delays in product launches.
- Solution: Utilized ChatGPT to create marketing content and campaign ideas.
- Results: Launched products 30% faster, increased social media engagement by 40%, and boosted sales by 25%.

Action Step:

Use ChatGPT to generate marketing content and campaign ideas, ensuring rapid and effective promotion of your new products.

Reflection Prompt:

How can leveraging ChatGPT for marketing content creation accelerate your product launch timelines and enhance your promotional efforts?

3. Generating Creative Ideas

Overcoming Creative Blocks with AI

Creative blocks can hinder progress. ChatGPT is a brainstorming partner that provides a wealth of innovative ideas to inspire your team.

Benefits:

- Idea Generation: Offers a multitude of creative concepts.
- Diversity of Thought: Introduces varied perspectives and novel solutions.
- Efficiency: Speeds up the brainstorming process.

Example:

A game developer seeks new concepts for an educational game targeting middle school students.

Prompt: "Suggest innovative ideas for an educational game that teaches basic programming concepts to middle school students."

ChatGPT Response:

- It is a puzzle adventure where players solve coding challenges to progress.
- A virtual world where students build their games using drag-and-drop coding.
- A competitive coding tournament with real-time problem-solving.

Technical Insights:

ChatGPT leverages pattern recognition and knowledge from various creative domains to generate original ideas, assisting in overcoming creative stagnation.

Case Study: EduPlay Studios

- Challenge: Difficulty generating fresh game concepts.

- Solution: Employed ChatGPT for ideation sessions.
- Results: Developed a new game that increased user engagement by 35% and received educational awards.

Action Step:
Use ChatGPT to generate creative ideas, enhance your team's brainstorming sessions, and drive innovation.

Reflection Prompt:
How can using ChatGPT to generate creative ideas help your team overcome creative blocks and foster innovation?

4. Focusing on the Best Ideas

Prioritizing High-Potential Concepts with AI
With numerous ideas generated, it is crucial to identify the most promising ones. ChatGPT can assist by analyzing data and predicting potential success.

Benefits:
- Data-Driven Decisions: Objectively evaluates and prioritizes ideas.
- Resource Optimization: Focuses efforts on high-impact concepts.
- Improved Outcomes: Increases the likelihood of successful products.

Example:
A healthcare company wants to prioritize features for a new patient management system.
Prompt: "Based on current healthcare technology trends, which should be prioritized in a patient management system for small clinics?"

ChatGPT Response:
- Telemedicine capabilities for remote consultations.
- Secure patient data management with compliance with HIPAA regulations.
- User-friendly interface for staff with minimal training requirements.

Technical Insights:

ChatGPT can analyze trends and data patterns using its extensive training data, providing insights into which ideas may have the most significant impact or market acceptance.

Case Study: MediTech Solutions

- Challenge: Difficulty prioritizing features in a competitive market.
- Solution: Leveraged ChatGPT to analyze market needs and rank features.
- Results: Streamlined development focus, leading to a product that increased market share by 20%.

Action Step:

Leverage ChatGPT to analyze and prioritize your ideas, ensuring your team focuses on concepts with the highest potential for success.

Reflection Prompt:

How can utilizing ChatGPT to prioritize your ideas improve your decision-making process and product success rates?

5. Enhancing Team Collaboration

Improving Engagement and Communication with AI

Effective collaboration is critical to successful product development. ChatGPT can facilitate communication, making it easier for teams to share ideas and provide feedback.

Benefits:

- Streamlined Communication: Automates meeting notes and action items.
- Enhanced Collaboration: Encourages idea-sharing and collective problem-solving.
- Consistency: Keeps all team members informed and aligned.

Example:

A multinational team is working on a global marketing campaign. ChatGPT helps by summarizing meetings and translating key points.

Prompt: "Summarize today's meeting highlights and action items for the global marketing team and translate them into Spanish and Mandarin."

ChatGPT Response:

- Meeting Highlights:

   - Reviewed campaign timelines.
   - Discussed regional market strategies.
- Action Items:
   - Marketing Leads: Finalize regional plans by Friday.
   - Design Team: Submit ad creatives by next Wednesday.

Translations are provided accordingly.

Technical Insights:
ChatGPT's language capabilities, including summarization and translation, stem from its advanced NLP algorithms trained on multilingual data.

Case Study: GlobalReach Corp.

- Challenge: Communication barriers within a diverse, international team.
- Solution: Integrated ChatGPT for meeting summaries and translations.
- Results: Improved team alignment, reduced misunderstandings, and increased project efficiency by 25%.

Action Step:
Implement ChatGPT to automate communication tasks, enhancing team collaboration and productivity.

Reflection Prompt:
How can using ChatGPT to facilitate communication and collaboration improve your team's effectiveness?

6. Planning for the Future with AI Insights

Taking Future-Proof Initiatives
Staying ahead requires foresight. ChatGPT can help analyze emerging trends, technologies, and consumer behaviors to inform strategic planning.

Benefits:

- Strategic Planning: Provides insights into future market conditions.
- Informed Decisions: Supports decisions with predictive analysis.

- Competitive Edge: Identifies opportunities and threats early.

Example:
An automotive company is exploring the future of electric vehicles.
Prompt: "What are the emerging consumer preferences and technological advancements in electric vehicles over the next five years?"

ChatGPT Response:

- Increased demand for longer battery life and faster charging.
- Integration with smart home and IoT devices.
- Autonomous driving features are becoming standard.

Technical Insights:
ChatGPT can synthesize information from various sources to identify trends and make educated predictions about future developments.

Case Study: DriveForward Motors

- Challenge: Uncertainty about future consumer preferences.
- Solution: Used ChatGPT for strategic forecasting.
- Results: Aligned R&D with future trends, leading to innovative products that captured new market segments.

Action Step:
Use ChatGPT to analyze trends and plan strategically, ensuring your initiatives are future-proof.

Reflection Prompt:
How can leveraging AI insights help you anticipate market changes and adapt your strategies?

7. Streamlining Market Research

Reviewing and Analyzing Data Faster with AI
Market research is essential but time-consuming. ChatGPT can expedite this process by quickly analyzing data and summarizing key insights.

Benefits:

- Speed: Delivers insights rapidly.
- Comprehensive Analysis: Handles large datasets efficiently.
- Actionable Insights: Provides clear summaries for decision-making.

Example:

A retail company needs to understand customer feedback from thousands of reviews.
Prompt: "Summarize common customer sentiments from these product reviews."

ChatGPT Response:

- Customers appreciate product quality but desire faster shipping.
- Frequent requests for more size and color options.
- Positive feedback on customer service responsiveness.

Technical Insights:

ChatGPT's ability to perform sentiment analysis and summarization comes from its training in NLP tasks, enabling it to process and interpret large volumes of text data.

Case Study: ShopEase Retail

- Challenge: Overwhelmed by customer feedback data.
- Solution: Implemented ChatGPT for data analysis.
- Results: Identified critical areas for improvement, leading to enhanced customer satisfaction and increased repeat business.

Action Step:

Deploy ChatGPT to streamline your market research process, gaining timely insights to inform your strategies.

Reflection Prompt:

How can using ChatGPT to analyze market data improve your responsiveness to customer needs?

8. Upholding High Standards of Innovation

Ensuring Excellence in Product Development with AI

Quality and innovation go hand in hand. ChatGPT can help evaluate product concepts, simulate scenarios, and suggest optimizations, ensuring your products meet the highest standards before launch.

Benefits:

- Continuous Improvement: Facilitates ongoing refinement of ideas.
- Quality Assurance: Identifies potential issues early.
- Risk Mitigation: Reduces the likelihood of costly post-launch fixes.

Example:

A pharmaceutical company wants to ensure the safety and efficacy of a new drug.

Prompt: "Simulate potential side effects and interactions of this new drug based on known data."

ChatGPT Response:

- Possible mild side effects include nausea and headache.
- Potential interactions with blood pressure medications.
- Recommend further clinical trials focusing on patients with cardiovascular conditions.

Technical Insights:

While ChatGPT cannot replace clinical trials, it can process existing medical data to identify areas of concern, aiding in preliminary assessments.

Case Study: HealthFirst Pharmaceuticals

- Challenge: Need for early detection of potential drug issues.
- Solution: ChatGPT was used to analyze data and simulate scenarios.
- Results: Identified key trial focus areas, improving drug safety and compliance.

Action Step:

Implement ChatGPT to evaluate and refine your products, ensuring they meet high innovation and quality standards.

Reflection Prompt:

How can using AI to uphold high standards enhance your product's success and reputation?

9. Launching Game-Changing Products

Bringing Innovative Solutions to Market with AI

ChatGPT can assist in developing and promoting groundbreaking products, giving businesses a competitive edge.

Benefits:

- Competitive Advantage: Accelerates innovation and time-to-market.
- Scalability: Supports growth efficiently.
- Enhanced Promotion: Creates effective marketing strategies.

Example:

A renewable energy startup aims to disrupt the market with a new solar technology.

Prompt: "Develop a go-to-market strategy for a cost-effective, high-efficiency solar panel targeting urban homeowners."

ChatGPT Response:

- Marketing Channels: Social media campaigns highlighting cost savings.
- Partnerships: Collaborate with home improvement retailers.
- Incentives: Offer installation discounts and highlight tax credits.

Technical Insights:

ChatGPT can synthesize business strategies by combining market analysis, consumer behavior, and effective promotional tactics.

Case Study: SunPower Innovations

- Challenge: Limited resources to market a new solar product.
- Solution: Used ChatGPT for strategic planning and content creation.
- Results: Successfully penetrated the market, achieving significant sales growth and attracting investor interest.

Action Step:

Leverage ChatGPT throughout the product lifecycle to bring innovative solutions to market effectively.

Reflection Prompt:
How can integrating AI into your product development and marketing strategies drive the success of your innovative products?

Conclusion: Embracing AI for Accelerated Product Development

Embracing AI in product development transforms how businesses innovate and compete. ChatGPT is a powerful ally that enhances efficiency, fosters creativity, and ensures products meet the highest standards. By integrating AI thoughtfully, you can navigate the complexities of product development with greater ease and success.

Key Takeaways:

- AI as a Collaborative Tool: Use AI to augment human creativity and decision-making.
- Efficiency and Precision: Automate tasks to focus on strategic initiatives.
- Data-Driven Insights: Inform decisions with comprehensive analysis.
- Ethical Considerations: Ensure AI use promotes fairness and transparency.
- Continuous Adaptation: Stay updated with AI advancements to maintain a competitive edge.

Action Steps:

1. Implement AI Tools: Start integrating ChatGPT into various stages of your product development process.
2. Customize Strategies: Tailor AI applications to meet your specific needs and objectives.
3. Foster Innovation: Encourage your team to leverage AI for creative imagination.
4. Optimize Workflows: Use AI to streamline processes and reduce time-to-market.
5. Invest in Training: Equip your team with the skills to use AI effectively.

Reflection Prompt:

Consider your current product development challenges. How can integrating AI tools like ChatGPT address these challenges and enhance your innovation capabilities?

Chapter 12: Strategy 10 – Automating Language Translation

Expanding Your Business Globally with AI-Powered Translation

Imagine you're running an organization eager to tap into international markets or serve a diverse clientele. The potential for growth and impact is immense, but language barriers stand in your way. Communicating effectively with a global audience feels daunting, with endless documents needing translation and cultural nuances. Then, you discover AI-powered language translation—specifically, tools like ChatGPT—and suddenly, global communication becomes seamless. It's like having a team of expert linguists available 24/7, ready to bridge the gap between languages and cultures.

1. The Importance of Language Translation in Global Operations

Breaking Down Barriers with AI

In today's interconnected world, language should no longer be a barrier to expansion or service delivery. Effective communication is vital to building relationships with international clients, partners, students, patients, and beneficiaries. AI-powered language translation enables entities across various sectors—healthcare, education, non-profits, or businesses—to communicate across borders effortlessly, opening doors to new opportunities and making services more accessible.

Benefits:

- Global Reach: Access markets or communities previously out of reach due to language limitations.
- Cost Efficiency: Reduce the expenses associated with traditional translation services.
- Speed: Translate large volumes of content quickly to keep up with fast-paced global demands.

Example:

A healthcare organization aims to provide telemedicine services to non-English-speaking patients. Using AI-powered translation, they can offer medical consultations, patient education materials, and follow-up care instructions in multiple languages, ensuring that language is not a barrier to quality healthcare.

Case Study: GlobalHealth Telemedicine

- Challenge: Inability to effectively communicate with a diverse patient population.
- Solution: Implemented ChatGPT-powered translation to provide multilingual telehealth services.
- Results: Expanded patient base by 35%, improved patient satisfaction, and enhanced health outcomes through better communication.

Action Step:

Evaluate your organization's content and communication channels to identify areas where AI-powered tools like ChatGPT can automate and enhance translation efforts.

Reflection Prompt:

How can automating language translation accelerate your organization's global initiatives and improve communication with diverse stakeholders?

2. How AI-Powered Language Translation Works

Understanding the Technology Behind the Tool

AI-powered translation leverages Natural Language Processing (NLP) and machine learning algorithms to interpret and translate text from one language to another. These models are trained on extensive multilingual datasets, enabling them to understand context, syntax, and semantics specific to various industries.

Technical Insights:

- Neural Machine Translation (NMT): Uses deep learning to produce more natural-sounding translations by considering entire sentences rather than a word-for-word translation.
- Domain Adaptation: AI models can be fine-tuned with industry-specific data to improve accuracy in specialized fields like medical or legal terminology.
- Continuous Learning: The AI improves by learning from new data inputs and user feedback.

Example:
An educational institution offering online courses uses ChatGPT to translate course content into multiple languages. The AI model is trained with academic terminology to maintain the integrity of educational materials across different languages.

Action Step:
Understand how AI models like ChatGPT process language translation in your specific sector to implement and customize these tools for your needs effectively.

Reflection Prompt:
Which technical aspects of AI-powered translation are most relevant to your field, and how can a more profound understanding enhance your implementation strategy?

3. Implementing AI-Powered Translation in Your Sector

Steps to Seamless Global Communication
Integrating AI-powered translation into your operations involves selecting suitable tools, customizing them for your industry, and ensuring smooth integration with existing systems.

Implementation Guide:

1. Assess Translation Needs:
    - Identify content types requiring translation (e.g., patient information in healthcare, curriculum in education, donor communications in non-profits).
    - Determine target languages based on your audience or service areas.
2. Select the Right AI Tool:
    - Evaluate tools like ChatGPT for their language capabilities and compatibility with your systems.
    - Consider whether the tool supports domain-specific customization.
3. Customize for Industry-Specific Terminology:
    - Train the AI model with industry-specific vocabulary and jargon.
    - Develop glossaries and style guides to enhance translation accuracy.
4. Integrate with Existing Systems:

- Connect the AI tool to your content management, learning management, or patient record systems.
- Automate translation workflows to increase efficiency.

5. Quality Assurance:
   - Implement a review process involving industry experts or native speakers.
   - Collect feedback to improve the AI model's performance continuously.

Case Study: EduConnect International

- Challenge: Difficulty providing educational content to international students due to language barriers.
- Solution: Integrated ChatGPT to translate and localize online course materials.
- Results: Increased international student enrollment by 50%, improved student satisfaction, and broadened global reach.

Action Step:

Create a detailed plan for integrating AI-powered translation into your operations, tailored to your industry's requirements.

Reflection Prompt:

What steps can you take to ensure the effective implementation of AI-powered translation in your sector?

4. Enhancing Client and Stakeholder Engagement with Multilingual Support

Providing Exceptional Service Globally

Offering services in clients' or stakeholders' native languages enhances their experience and fosters more robust relationships. AI-powered translation tools enable real-time multilingual communication without extensive language resources.

Benefits:

- Inclusivity: Make services accessible to a broader audience.
- Efficiency: Provide timely responses in multiple languages.
- Trust Building: Show respect and understanding of cultural and linguistic diversity.

Example:

A non-profit organization in disaster relief uses ChatGPT to communicate with affected communities in their native languages, ensuring timely and effective aid delivery.

Case Study: ReliefAid International

- Challenge: Language barriers hinder effective communication during international disaster response.
- Solution: Deployed ChatGPT to translate emergency communication and aid instructions.
- Results: Improved response times, enhanced coordination with local partners, and increased aid effectiveness.

Action Step:

Incorporate AI-powered translation into your client or stakeholder communication strategies to enhance engagement and service delivery.

Reflection Prompt:

How can offering multilingual support improve your organization's relationships and impact in your sector?

5. Localizing Content and Services with AI

Culturally Relevant Adaptations

Beyond translation, localization involves adapting content to align with cultural norms and preferences. AI-powered tools can assist in creating materials and services that resonate with local audiences.

Benefits:

- Cultural Relevance: Ensure content is appropriate and engaging for different cultures.
- Market Penetration: Increase acceptance and effectiveness of services or products in new regions.
- Brand Consistency: Maintain your organization's voice and messaging across languages.

Example:

An educational publisher uses ChatGPT to localize textbooks, incorporating region-specific examples and cultural references to enhance student engagement.

Case Study: LearnWell Publishing

- Challenge: Limited adoption of educational materials in international markets.
- Solution: Utilized AI-powered translation and localization to adapt content for different regions.
- Results: Expanded global market share by 45%, improved educational outcomes, and received positive feedback from educators worldwide.

Action Step:
Leverage AI-powered translation to localize your organization's content and services, ensuring they are culturally appropriate and effective.

Reflection Prompt:
What cultural considerations are important in your field, and how can AI assist in localizing your offerings to meet these needs?

6. Facilitating Multilingual Collaboration

Enhancing Teamwork Across Borders
Effective multilingual communication is vital for organizations with international teams. AI-powered translation can bridge language gaps, fostering better collaboration and innovation.

Benefits:

- Improved Communication: Reduce misunderstandings and streamline project workflows.
- Inclusive Environment: Create a sense of unity among diverse team members.
- Innovation: Leverage diverse perspectives for creative problem-solving.

Example:
A research consortium involving scientists from various countries uses ChatGPT to translate research papers, collaborative documents, and meeting transcripts, ensuring the alignment of all team members.

Case Study: Global Research Network

- Challenge: Language differences slow down collaborative research efforts.
- Solution: Implemented AI translation for all collaborative communications.
- Results: Accelerated research timelines, increased publication output, and fostered a cohesive international team.

Action Step:
Integrate AI-powered translation into your collaboration tools to enhance communication among international teams.

Reflection Prompt:
How can improved multilingual collaboration benefit your organization's goals and innovation capacity?

7. Expanding Reach in Healthcare and Education

Improving Access and Outcomes
Language barriers can significantly impact service delivery and outcomes in sectors like healthcare and education. AI-powered translation can enhance access to essential services.

Benefits:

- Patient Care: Ensure patients understand medical information, leading to better health outcomes.
- Educational Equity: Provide learning materials in students' native languages, improving comprehension and success rates.
- Community Engagement: Build stronger relationships with diverse populations.

Example:
A university uses ChatGPT to translate admission materials and course catalogs, attracting a more diverse student body and promoting inclusivity.

Case Study: Unity University

- Challenge: Underrepresentation of international students due to language barriers.
- Solution: Translated recruitment materials and online resources using AI-powered tools.
- Results: Increased international student enrollment by 30%, enhanced campus

diversity, and enriched the learning environment.

Action Step:
Apply AI-powered translation to expand access and improve outcomes in your healthcare or educational services.

Reflection Prompt:
In what ways can AI-assisted translation enhance service delivery and equity in your sector?

8. Ensuring Accuracy and Compliance in Legal and Technical Translations

Maintaining High Standards in Specialized Fields
Accuracy is crucial when translating legal documents, technical manuals, or compliance materials. AI-powered translation can assist, but it must be complemented by expert review.

Best Practices:

- Expert Involvement: Have professionals validate AI translations.
- Customized Training: Use domain-specific data to train the AI model.
- Compliance Checks: Ensure translations meet legal and regulatory standards.

Example:
An engineering firm uses ChatGPT to translate technical manuals for international clients, with engineers reviewing them to ensure precision.

Case Study: TechSolutions Engineering

- Challenge: High costs and delays in producing multilingual technical documentation.
- Solution: Implemented AI translation with expert validation.
- Results: Reduced documentation production time by 50%, decreased costs, and improved client satisfaction.

Action Step:
Incorporate AI-powered translation in your technical or legal documentation processes, ensuring accuracy through expert oversight.

Reflection Prompt:
What steps can you take to ensure AI-assisted translations meet the stringent requirements of your specialized field?

9. Ethical Considerations and Cultural Sensitivity in AI Translation

Promoting Responsible Use
Ethical considerations are paramount when using AI for language translation. Potential biases must be addressed, and cultural sensitivity must be ensured.

Guidelines:

- Bias Awareness: Regularly evaluate AI outputs for unintended biases.
- Cultural Respect: Ensure translations are culturally appropriate and sensitive.
- Transparency: Inform stakeholders about the use of AI in communications when necessary.

Example:
A non-profit working with vulnerable populations implements strict guidelines for AI translation, including regular audits and involving community representatives in reviewing materials.

Action Step:
Develop and implement ethical policies for AI translation use, focusing on fairness, respect, and accountability.

Reflection Prompt:
How can you ensure your AI translation aligns with ethical standards and respects the cultures you engage with?

Conclusion: Leveraging AI-Powered Translation for Global Advancement

Embracing AI-powered language translation unlocks new possibilities for organizations across various sectors. By enhancing communication and breaking down language barriers, you can expand your reach, improve services, and significantly impact globally.

Key Takeaways:

- Strategic Adoption: Thoughtfully integrate AI translation tools tailored to your sector.

- Human-AI Synergy: Combine AI efficiency with human expertise for high-quality outcomes.
- Continuous Learning: Stay informed about technological advancements to maintain a competitive edge.
- Ethical Commitment: Uphold ethical standards and cultural sensitivity in all AI-assisted communications.

Action Steps:

1. Identify Opportunities: Pinpoint areas where language translation can significantly enhance your operations or services.
2. Select Appropriate Tools: Choose AI translation solutions that meet your industry's needs.
3. Customize and Integrate: Tailor the tools to your specific context and integrate them smoothly into existing workflows.
4. Establish Ethical Guidelines: Develop policies to govern the responsible use of AI translation.
5. Monitor Effectiveness: Continuously assess the impact and refine your approach based on feedback and outcomes.

Reflection Prompt:

Consider the potential impact of AI-powered language translation on your organization's mission and goals. What immediate steps can you take to begin this transformative journey?

Additional Resources:

- AI Translation Platforms: OpenAI's ChatGPT API, Microsoft Translator, Amazon Translate
- Industry-Specific NLP Courses: "AI for Medicine" by Coursera, "NLP with Deep Learning" by Stanford University
- Ethical AI Frameworks: "The Montreal Declaration for Responsible AI," IEEE's "Ethically Aligned Design"
- Professional Communities: AI in Healthcare forums, Educational Technology groups on LinkedIn, Non-Profit Technology Network (NTEN)

Chapter 13: Strategy 11 – Optimizing SEO Strategies

Have You Ever Wished Keyword Research Could Be as Easy as Waving a Magic Wand?

With ChatGPT, it's almost that simple! Imagine a world where you just type in a few prompts, sit back with your coffee, and voilà! Your comprehensive keyword strategy is ready before you say "search engine optimization."

The Game-Changer: ChatGPT for Keyword Research

Before ChatGPT, keyword research felt like a Herculean task. You'd spend hours, if not days, sifting through data. Now, enter a few commands into ChatGPT and watch the magic unfold. However, remember that ChatGPT's knowledge is capped at 2021. Many businesses turn to tools like Gemini, which keeps pace with the ever-changing internet landscape for the freshest data.

1. Step-by-Step: Using ChatGPT for Keyword Research

a. Input Your Topic

Start by entering a broad topic or phrase related to your niche—for example, type "healthy recipes" into ChatGPT.

b. Generate Keyword List

Ask ChatGPT to generate a list of relevant keywords.

Command: "Generate a list of keywords for healthy recipes."

c. Filter High-Volume Keywords

Refine the list by requesting high-volume keywords.

Command: "Show only keywords with high search volume."

d. Customize and Expand

Personalize the list further by asking for variations or long-tail keywords.

Command: "Expand on these keywords with long-tail variations."

Example:

For a fitness blog, you might start with "workout routines." ChatGPT can quickly provide a list of high-traffic keywords like "beginner workout routines," "home workout routines," and "quick workout routines."

Case Study: FitLife Blog

- Challenge: Low organic traffic due to ineffective keyword strategies.
- Solution: Implemented ChatGPT for comprehensive keyword research.
- Results: Increased organic traffic by 40% and improved search engine rankings for targeted keywords within three months.

Action Step: Use ChatGPT to generate and refine a list of keywords for your niche. Implement these keywords into your content to enhance SEO performance.

Reflection Prompt: How can refining your keyword strategy with ChatGPT improve your website's visibility and attract more targeted traffic?

2. Speeding Up Competitive Keyword Research

Let's face it: online tools for keyword research can be a time sink. Even Google Ads' Keyword Planner demands a fair bit of elbow grease. But with ChatGPT, you can generate a long list of keywords, each tailored to specific search intents, faster than you can say "search volume."

Generate, Customize, Cleanup, and Expand Keyword Lists

Think of ChatGPT as your SEO fairy godmother. Need a list of high-volume keywords? Done. Want to tweak them to fit your niche better? Easy. ChatGPT can even generate similar keywords you might overlook, all while you relax with a nice cup of tea.

Brainstorming Keywords Across Different Topics

Do you have a simple topic? Great! Have a complex one? Even better! ChatGPT can handle it all, helping you easily rank primary, secondary, and long-tail keywords. You can even ask it to generate LSI (Latent Semantic Indexing) keywords, making your SEO strategy as robust as possible.

Example Use Case:

- Simple Topic: For a blog on "yoga for beginners," you might start with primary keywords. ChatGPT can help expand this to include "beginner yoga poses," "yoga for flexibility," and "easy yoga routines."

- Complex Topic: For a tech blog focusing on “AI in healthcare,” ChatGPT can generate a diverse set of keywords such as “AI healthcare applications,” “machine learning in medical diagnostics,” and “AI health tech trends.”

Action Step: Utilize ChatGPT to brainstorm a wide range of keywords for simple and complex topics, ensuring a comprehensive and competitive SEO strategy.

Reflection Prompt: How can leveraging ChatGPT for competitive keyword research give your SEO strategy an edge over competitors?

3. Create an Engaging FAQ Section

A well-crafted FAQ section can boost engagement and make your content more user-friendly. But who has the time to create all those questions and answers? ChatGPT does!

Step-by-Step: Creating a FAQ Section

1. Identify Common Questions: Input a prompt such as, "What are common questions about pasta dishes?"

2. Generate Answers: Ask ChatGPT to provide concise answers.

    - Command: "Generate answers for these questions."

3. Review and Personalize: Tweak the answers to align with your brand's voice and add any specific details.

Example:

For a tech blog, you might ask ChatGPT, "What are common questions about cloud computing?" ChatGPT can generate questions like "What is cloud computing?" and "How does cloud computing work?" along with detailed answers.

Case Study: TechInsight Blog

- Challenge: Low user engagement and high bounce rates.

- Solution: Created an engaging FAQ section using ChatGPT.

- Results: Reduced bounce rates by 25% and increased time spent on site by 30%.

Action Step: Use ChatGPT to generate a comprehensive FAQ section for your website, addressing common customer queries and enhancing user experience.

Reflection Prompt: How can incorporating AI-generated FAQs with ChatGPT enhance your website's user experience and improve SEO rankings?

4. Crafting Catchy Meta Titles and Descriptions

Want to boost your search engine rankings with killer meta titles and descriptions? Just ask ChatGPT. It can generate catchy, conversational titles and descriptions that match your brand's voice and elevate your SEO game.

Step-by-Step: Crafting Meta Titles and Descriptions

1. Input Your Topic: Enter the topic or article title.
2. Generate Meta Titles: Ask ChatGPT to create engaging meta titles.
    - Command: "Generate catchy meta titles for [topic]."
3. Generate Meta Descriptions: Request concise, engaging descriptions.
    - Command: "Generate meta descriptions for [topic]."
4. Review and Tweak: Adjust the generated text to match your brand's tone better.

Example:

For an article about the 10 Best Hiking Trails, you could ask ChatGPT to generate meta titles like "Explore the Top 10 Hiking Trails" and meta descriptions like "Discover the best hiking trails for adventure and breathtaking views."

Case Study: AdventureSeekers Blog

- Challenge: Low click-through rates (CTR) from search engine results pages (SERPs).
- Solution: Crafted optimized meta titles and descriptions using ChatGPT.
- Results: Increased CTR by 20% and improved rankings for targeted keywords.

Action Step: Utilize ChatGPT to generate and refine your meta titles and descriptions, ensuring they are engaging and SEO-friendly.

Reflection Prompt: How can crafting personalized meta titles and descriptions with ChatGPT improve your website's visibility and CTR?

5. Dominating Search Engine Rankings

To truly dominate Google, you need a multifaceted SEO strategy. ChatGPT can help you cut through the cobwebs of SEO complexities and focus on what matters most: creating original, engaging content. Feed it the correct information; ChatGPT will help you shine on the SERPs.

The Final Touch: Personalization

While ChatGPT is powerful, it's not infallible. Always add a personal touch to its suggestions to ensure your content stands out. Double-check facts and infuse your unique brand voice to create content that ranks high and resonates with your audience.

Best Practices:

- Fact-Checking: Ensure all information is accurate and up-to-date.
- Brand Voice: Customize the tone and style to align with your brand identity.
- Unique Insights: Add personal experiences or unique perspectives to differentiate your content.

Case Study: HealthPlus Clinic

- Challenge: Low organic traffic despite high-quality services.
- Solution: Implemented ChatGPT to create personalized, SEO-optimized blog content.
- Results: Increased organic traffic by 50% and improved patient inquiries through the website.

Action Step: Combine ChatGPT's content generation capabilities with your unique insights to create personalized and high-ranking content.

Reflection Prompt: How can personalizing AI-generated content with your unique brand voice enhance its effectiveness and SEO performance?

Conclusion: Dominating SEO with ChatGPT

Optimizing SEO strategies with ChatGPT is like having a secret weapon in your digital marketing arsenal. It simplifies complex tasks, enhances keyword research, and helps create engaging content that resonates with your audience. By thoughtfully integrating AI into your SEO efforts, you can achieve higher search engine rankings, increased organic traffic, and improved conversion rates.

Key Takeaways:

- AI is a Tool, Not a Replacement: Combine AI capabilities with human creativity to produce compelling and authentic content.
- Quality Over Quantity: Focus on creating valuable, engaging interactions that resonate with your audience.
- Ethics Matter: Uphold transparency, integrity, and fairness in all AI-assisted SEO strategies.
- Strategic Integration: Implement ChatGPT thoughtfully to maximize benefits and ensure seamless integration with existing systems.
- Continuous Learning: Stay updated with AI advancements and refine your SEO strategies to stay competitive.

Action Steps:

1. Implement AI Tools:
    - Start using ChatGPT for brainstorming, content creation, and keyword research to streamline your SEO workflow.
2. Optimize for SEO:
    - Utilize ChatGPT to enhance your content with SEO-friendly keywords, meta titles, and descriptions.
3. Monetize Thoughtfully:
    - Explore and integrate monetization strategies that align with your content and audience needs.
4. Maintain Ethical Standards:
    - Establish guidelines to ensure your AI-generated content remains accurate, original, and unbiased.
5. Continuous Learning:
    - Stay updated with AI advancements and continuously refine your SEO strategies to stay competitive.

Reflection Prompt:

Consider a recent content project you worked on. How could AI have improved your process? Reflect on balancing AI assistance and your creative input to enhance efficiency and quality.

Additional Resources:

- AI Integration Tools: Zapier, HubSpot, Salesforce Einstein
- NLP Learning Platforms: Coursera NLP Courses, edX NLP Programs
- Community Forums: Engage with other users on platforms like Reddit's r/OpenAI and LinkedIn Groups
- Ethical AI Guidelines: OpenAI's Responsible AI Practices

By thoughtfully integrating ChatGPT into your SEO strategies, you're not just adopting a new tool but transforming how you approach search engine optimization. Embrace the possibilities, stay informed about the latest AI advancements, and continuously refine your strategies to achieve exceptional SEO results. Remember, the goal is to utilize AI and blend its capabilities with human ingenuity to create content that stands out and ranks high.

Chapter 14: Strategy 12 – ChatGPT-Powered Virtual Assistants

Increasing Productivity with AI Support

Imagine having a highly efficient assistant who never sleeps, doesn't need breaks, and is always ready to help with any task. This isn't a futuristic dream—it's the reality of ChatGPT-powered virtual assistants. These AI-driven helpers are revolutionizing how businesses operate, enhancing productivity, and enabling teams to achieve their goals faster.

Contrary to some misconceptions, ChatGPT and other advanced language models aren't here to replace human jobs. Instead, they are potent tools that augment human capabilities, especially in media, technology, customer service, and beyond. Business leaders and managers recognize ChatGPT as a catalyst for efficiency, innovation, and growth. Say goodbye to outdated productivity methods—ChatGPT is here to elevate your operations to the next level.

1. Transforming Customer Support

AI-Powered Chatbots for 24/7 Service

Customer support is a critical aspect of any business, but maintaining a large support team can be costly and challenging. ChatGPT-powered chatbots offer an efficient and cost-effective solution by providing immediate, personalized responses to customer inquiries around the clock.

Benefits:

- Cost Reduction: Decrease expenditure on customer support staffing.
- Enhanced Availability: Offer 24/7 support, improving customer satisfaction.
- Consistency: Ensure uniform and accurate responses to customer queries.
- Scalability: Handle multiple customer interactions simultaneously without additional costs.

Technical Insights:

ChatGPT uses Natural Language Processing (NLP) to understand and generate human-like responses. It can interpret customer inquiries, even those phrased unconventionally, and provide relevant information or solutions.

Example:

A mid-sized e-commerce company implements a ChatGPT-powered chatbot to handle customer inquiries about order status, return policies, and product information. The chatbot provides instant responses, freeing human agents to focus on more complex issues.

Case Study: TechSolutions Inc.

- Challenge: High volume of customer inquiries leading to long wait times and decreased customer satisfaction.
- Solution: Integrated a ChatGPT-powered chatbot into their customer support system.
- Results:
    - We have reduced the average response time from 24 hours to under 2 minutes.
    - It decreased support costs by 50%.
    - We achieved a 30% increase in customer satisfaction ratings.

Action Step:

Integrate a ChatGPT-powered chatbot into your customer support channels to handle routine inquiries efficiently. Ensure the chatbot is trained on your company's knowledge base and frequently asked questions for optimal performance.

Reflection Prompt:

How can automating customer support with ChatGPT improve your customer experience and allow your team to focus on high-priority tasks?

2. Boosting Workplace Efficiency

Leveraging ChatGPT Across Business Functions

ChatGPT is not limited to customer support; it can enhance productivity across various departments. Here are several ways you can utilize ChatGPT to optimize your business operations:

a. Generating Creative Content

Enhance Marketing and Social Media Engagement

Use ChatGPT to create engaging and original content for marketing campaigns, social media posts, and promotional materials. Whether you need a captivating slogan, a compelling product description, or an entertaining blog post, ChatGPT can assist.

Example:

- Prompt: "Write a humorous social media post promoting our new eco-friendly water bottle."

- ChatGPT Response: "Say goodbye to single-use plastics and hello to hydration with a conscience! Our eco-friendly water bottle keeps your drink cool and the planet cooler. #SipSustainably"

b. Summarizing Reports and Documents

Save Time on Information Processing

ChatGPT can quickly summarize lengthy reports, articles, or meeting notes, highlighting key points and action items. This allows team members to grasp essential information without spending hours reading.

Example:

- Prompt: "Summarize the main findings of this 20-page market research report."

- ChatGPT Response: A concise summary outlining market trends, consumer preferences, and strategic recommendations.

c. Facilitating Brainstorming Sessions

Stimulate Innovation and Idea Generation

ChatGPT can be a virtual brainstorming partner when your team needs fresh ideas, suggesting innovative concepts and solutions.

Example:

- Prompt: "Suggest ten creative promotional ideas for our upcoming product launch."

- ChatGPT Response: It offers ideas like hosting a virtual launch event, collaborating with influencers, and creating interactive online experiences.

d. Reviewing and Editing Content

Ensure High-Quality Communications

ChatGPT can assist in proofreading and editing documents, emails, or marketing materials, correcting grammatical errors, and improving clarity.

Example:

- Prompt: "Review this email draft for clarity and professionalism."

- ChatGPT Response: Provides an edited email version with improved phrasing and tone.

e. Conducting Preliminary Research

Accelerate Information Gathering

You can use ChatGPT to gather information on various topics, compile lists, or summarize data, speeding up the research phase of projects.

Example:

- Prompt: "Provide an overview of the latest advancements in renewable energy technology."

- ChatGPT Response: Summarizes recent developments in solar, wind, and hydroelectric power, including emerging technologies.

Note: For academic or highly specialized research, always verify information with reliable sources, as ChatGPT's knowledge may include only some recent data.

f. Automating Administrative Tasks

Streamline Routine Operations

ChatGPT can handle administrative duties such as scheduling meetings, setting reminders, or organizing tasks.

Example:

- Prompt: "Create a meeting agenda for our quarterly sales review."

- ChatGPT Response: Generates an agenda outlining discussion points, time allocations, and participants.

g. Enhancing Training and Onboarding

Support Employee Development

Develop interactive training materials or FAQs for new employees using ChatGPT, ensuring they have access to essential information.

Example:

- Prompt: "Generate an FAQ document for new hires about our company's policies and procedures."

- ChatGPT Response: This lists common questions and answers about dress code, working hours, and company values.

h. Language Translation and Localization

Expand Global Reach

ChatGPT can translate documents, emails, and other content into multiple languages, facilitating communication with international clients and partners.
Example:

- Prompt: "Translate this product description into Spanish and French."
- ChatGPT Response: Provides accurate translations in the requested languages.

2. Personalizing Customer Interactions

Improve Marketing and Sales Outreach
Use ChatGPT to craft personalized messages for email campaigns, proposals, or customer follow-ups, increasing engagement and conversion rates.

Example:

- Prompt: "Compose a personalized follow-up email to a potential client who expressed interest in our software solution."
- ChatGPT Response: Drafts an email that addresses the client's specific needs and highlights the benefits of your product.

Case Study: GlobalTech Solutions

- Challenge: Overwhelmed staff due to repetitive administrative tasks and inefficient processes.
- Solution: Implemented ChatGPT to automate scheduling, report summarization, and content generation.
- Results:
  - I saved over 15 hours per week on administrative tasks.
  - It increased team productivity by 25%.
  - It improved employee satisfaction by reducing mundane workload.

Action Step:
Identify routine tasks within your organization that can be automated using ChatGPT. Implement the AI tool in these areas to enhance efficiency and allow your team to focus on strategic initiatives.

Reflection Prompt:

Which administrative or repetitive tasks consume significant time in your operations, and how can ChatGPT help streamline these processes?

3. Enhancing Collaboration and Communication

Fostering Teamwork with AI Assistance

Effective communication and collaboration are essential for team success. ChatGPT can facilitate these by providing tools and assistance that improve information sharing and project coordination.

a. Drafting and Editing Team Communications

Ensure Clarity and Professionalism

Use ChatGPT to compose or review emails, memos, and reports, ensuring they are clear, concise, and professional.

Example:

- Prompt: "Draft an email to the team announcing the new project management software rollout."

- ChatGPT Response: Provide a well-structured email outlining the new software's benefits, implementation timelines, and training resources.

b. Facilitating Virtual Meetings

Enhance Meeting Productivity

ChatGPT can help create meeting agendas, generate discussion points, and even summarize meeting notes for distribution.

Example:

- Prompt: "Summarize the key decisions and action items from today's marketing strategy meeting."

- ChatGPT Response: Provides a concise summary that can be shared with attendees.

c. Supporting Remote Work

Bridge Communication Gaps

For distributed teams, ChatGPT can help coordinate tasks, schedule across time zones, and maintain consistent communication.

Example:

- Prompt: "Create a collaborative task list for the product development team, prioritizing urgent items."

- ChatGPT Response: Generates a shared task list with priorities and deadlines.

Case Study: ConnectPlus

- Challenge: Communication breakdowns in a remote team environment, leading to project delays.
- Solution: Integrated ChatGPT will assist with coordination, scheduling, and documentation.
- Results:
  - Improved on-time project delivery by 35%.
  - Enhanced team collaboration and reduced miscommunication.
  - Increased overall team satisfaction.

Action Step:

Leverage ChatGPT to enhance communication within your team, mainly if operating remotely or across different locations.

Reflection Prompt:

How can improved communication and collaboration tools impact your team's productivity and project outcomes?

4. Supporting Decision-Making Processes

Utilizing AI for Data Analysis and Insights

Making informed decisions requires analyzing data and understanding trends. ChatGPT can help interpret data sets, generate reports, and provide insights that support strategic planning.

a. Data Interpretation and Visualization

Simplify Complex Information

ChatGPT can help interpret data by summarizing findings and suggesting visual representations like charts or graphs.

Example:

- Prompt: "Analyze this sales data and highlight key trends over the past quarter."
- ChatGPT Response: Summarizes sales performance, identifies top-selling products, and notes any significant changes.

b. Generating Business Reports

Streamline Reporting Processes

Automate the creation of regular reports by providing data inputs to ChatGPT and requesting a formatted report.

Example:

- Prompt: "Create a monthly performance report for the customer service department, including response times and customer satisfaction metrics."
- ChatGPT Response: Compiles the data into a structured report with critical metrics and insights.

c. Strategic Planning Support

Assist in Scenario Analysis

Use ChatGPT to explore potential outcomes of business decisions by inputting different variables and assessing possible impacts.

Example:

- Prompt: "Assess the potential market impact if we increase our product price by 10%."
- ChatGPT Response: Discusses possible effects on sales volume, revenue, customer perception, and competitor reactions.

Case Study: MarketMakers Corp.

- Challenge: Difficulty in quickly analyzing market data to make timely decisions.
- Solution: Implemented ChatGPT to assist with data analysis and report generation.
- Results:
  - Reduced decision-making time by 40%.
  - Made more informed strategic choices, leading to a 15% increase in market share.
  - Enhanced ability to respond to market changes promptly.

Action Step:

Incorporate ChatGPT into your data analysis and reporting workflows to enhance the speed and quality of your decision-making processes.

Reflection Prompt:

How can AI-assisted data analysis improve your ability to make strategic decisions and respond to market dynamics?

5. Ensuring Ethical and Responsible AI Use

Maintaining Trust and Compliance

While leveraging ChatGPT's capabilities, it's crucial to use the technology responsibly, adhering to ethical guidelines and ensuring compliance with relevant regulations.

Best Practices:

- Data Privacy: ChatGPT must ensure that any sensitive information processed is handled securely and complies with data protection laws.
- Bias Mitigation: Regularly review AI outputs to identify and correct any biases or inappropriate content.
- Transparency: Be open with stakeholders about using AI in your operations, fostering trust.

Example:

A company implements guidelines for AI use, including regular audits of ChatGPT's outputs and training for employees on responsible AI practices.

Action Step:

Develop and enforce ethical guidelines for using AI within your organization, including staff training and regular reviews of AI outputs.

Reflection Prompt:

What measures can you implement to ensure that your organization's use of ChatGPT meets its ethical standards and legal obligations?

Conclusion: Harnessing the Power of AI for Enhanced Productivity

Integrating ChatGPT-powered virtual assistants into business operations can significantly enhance productivity, efficiency, and innovation. ChatGPT is a valuable partner in achieving organizational goals by automating routine tasks, improving communication, and supporting decision-making. Embracing this technology thoughtfully and responsibly positions your business to thrive in an increasingly competitive and dynamic environment.

Key Takeaways:

- Augment Human Capabilities: Use ChatGPT to enhance, not replace, human effort.

- Optimize Operations: Automate routine tasks to save time and resources.
- Enhance Communication: Improve team collaboration and customer interactions.
- Support Strategic Decisions: Leverage AI for data analysis and insights.
- Ethical Use: Commit to responsible AI practices to maintain trust and compliance.

Action Steps:

1. Identify Opportunities: Assess areas where ChatGPT can add value to your organization.
2. Implement Thoughtfully: Integrate AI tools in a way that complements your workflows.
3. Train Your Team: Provide training on how to use ChatGPT effectively and responsibly.
4. Monitor and Adapt: Continuously evaluate the impact and make adjustments as needed.
5. Stay Informed: Keep up with AI advancements to leverage new capabilities.

Reflection Prompt:

Consider a time-consuming or resource-intensive process or task in your organization. How could ChatGPT-powered virtual assistants transform this aspect of your operations?

Additional Resources

- AI Integration Tools: Zapier, Microsoft Power Automate, IBM Watson Assistant
- NLP Learning Platforms: Coursera's "Natural Language Processing Specialization," Udemy's "ChatGPT Masterclass"
- Community Forums: OpenAI Community, AI Stack Exchange, LinkedIn AI Professionals Group
- Ethical AI Guidelines: "Ethics Guidelines for Trustworthy AI" by the European Commission, IEEE's "Ethically Aligned Design"

Final Thoughts

By thoughtfully integrating ChatGPT-powered virtual assistants into your operations, you are embracing a powerful tool that enhances productivity and innovation. The synergy between AI capabilities and human expertise can drive exceptional results, fostering a work environment that is efficient, creative, and forward-thinking. Stay proactive in learning and adapting to AI advancements to maintain a competitive edge and achieve sustained success.

Chapter 15: Strategy 13 – AI-Driven Email Campaigns

Crafting Engaging Email Content with ChatGPT

Email marketing remains a cornerstone of digital marketing due to its direct reach and high return on investment. Crafting compelling and personalized emails, however, can be time-consuming and challenging. ChatGPT, an advanced AI language model, revolutionizes this process by automating email creation, enhancing personalization, and improving overall campaign efficiency.

Why ChatGPT Transforms Email Marketing

Integrating ChatGPT into your email marketing strategy offers several key advantages:

- Efficiency: Automate the email creation process, saving valuable time and resources.
- Personalization: Generate tailored content that resonates with individual recipients.
- Versatility: Handle various emails, from promotional offers to sensitive communications.
- Scalability: Easily expand your email campaigns without compromising quality.

Example:

Imagine needing to send 500 personalized welcome emails for a new product launch. ChatGPT can generate these emails in minutes, each customized with the recipient's name and interests based on your data, enhancing engagement and conversion rates.

Understanding How ChatGPT Enhances Email Marketing

Technical Insights

ChatGPT leverages advanced natural language processing (NLP) and machine learning algorithms to generate human-like text based on input prompts. In the context of email marketing, ChatGPT can:

- Generate Content: Produce email drafts that align with your desired tone and style.
- Personalize Messages: Incorporate recipient-specific details to enhance relevance.
- Optimize Language: Craft compelling subject lines and calls-to-action (CTAs) that drive engagement.

Limitations and Considerations:

- Knowledge Cutoff: ChatGPT's training data extends up to 2021. Ensure time-sensitive content is up-to-date.
- Review Required: Always proofread AI-generated content for accuracy and appropriateness.
- Prompt Engineering: The output quality depends on the clarity and specificity of your prompts.

The Art of Writing Effective Emails with ChatGPT

Mimicking Your Writing Style

Train ChatGPT to reflect your brand's unique voice to maintain consistency across communications.

Best Practices:

- Provide Examples: Input samples of previous emails to guide the model.
- Specify Tone and Style: Clearly define whether the tone should be professional, friendly, formal, or casual.

Example Prompt:

"Using a friendly and professional tone, draft a welcome email for new subscribers that introduces our brand values and encourages engagement."

Creating Diverse and Engaging Content

Generate concise, personalized, and engaging emails that capture your audience's attention.

Tips:

- Personalization Tokens: Include recipient names and other personal details.
- Clarity and Brevity: Keep messages clear and to the point.
- Compelling CTAs: Use robust and action-oriented language to encourage responses.

Example:
Instead of a generic greeting, use: "Hi [Name], we're excited to introduce you to our latest features!"

Automating Unique Elements

Automate the creation of subject lines, greetings, and supportive sentences to enhance engagement.

Practical Use:

- Subject Lines: Ask ChatGPT to generate multiple options and select the most effective one.
- Greetings: Customize openings to match the recipient's profile or preferences.

Types of Emails You Can Create with ChatGPT

1. Promotional Emails
Objective: Drive sales and engagement with compelling offers.
Strategies:

- Engaging Content: Highlight benefits and unique selling points without sounding robotic.
- A/B Testing: Experiment with different subject lines, images, and CTAs.

Example:

- Subject Line A: "Exclusive Offer: Upgrade Your Experience Today!"
- Subject Line B: "Discover the New Features Everyone's Talking About"

2. Cold Sales Emails

Objective: Initiate personal contact with potential clients.
Strategies:

- Personalized Touches: Address specific pain points relevant to the recipient.
- Clear Value Proposition: Explain how your solution meets their needs.

Example:
"Hi [Name], I noticed your company is expanding in [industry]. Our solutions can help streamline your operations and reduce costs."

3. Congratulatory Emails
Objective: Build relationships by acknowledging achievements or milestones.
Strategies:

- Genuine Tone: Convey heartfelt congratulations.
- Supportive Language: Express enthusiasm for their success.

Example:
"Congratulations on your recent award! We're proud to partner with industry leaders like you."

4. Thank You Emails
Objective: Strengthen relationships post-transaction.
Strategies:

- Personal Touches: Reference the specific purchase or interaction.
- Future Engagement: Encourage continued collaboration.

Example:
"Thank you for choosing us for your [service/product]. We appreciate your trust and look forward to serving you again."

5. Pitch Emails
Objective: Present proposals effectively to boost conversion rates.
Strategies:

- Address Needs: Tailor your message to the recipient's specific challenges.
- Time Efficiency: Deliver concise and impactful pitches.

Example:
"We have a solution that can improve your team's productivity by 25%. Let's discuss how we can implement this for your organization."

6. Polite and Sincere Emails

Objective: Communicate with professionalism and empathy.

Strategies:

- Appropriate Tone: Balance professionalism with warmth.
- Clarity: Be clear about the purpose while showing respect.

Example:

"We apologize for any inconvenience caused and appreciate your understanding as we work to resolve this issue promptly."

Enhancing Email Performance with ChatGPT

A/B Testing for Optimization

Use ChatGPT to create different versions of your emails to determine which performs better.

Implementation:

- Subject Lines: Generate multiple options and test for open rates.
- Content Layout: Experiment with different structures and messaging styles.

Example:

- CTA Version A: "Sign up for our webinar now!"
- CTA Version B: "Join our exclusive webinar today and gain valuable insights."

Crafting Compelling Calls-to-Action (CTAs)

Generate CTAs that drive engagement and conversions.

Tips:

- Action-Oriented Language: Use strong verbs to prompt action.
- Benefit Highlighting: Emphasize what the recipient gains.

Example:

"Download your free guide now and start optimizing your strategy today!"

Prompt Replies and Automated Responses

Automate responses to incoming emails to maintain prompt communication.

Use Case:

- Common Inquiries: Set up ChatGPT to generate responses for frequently asked questions.
- Personalization: Customize replies to reflect the sender's inquiry.

Best Practices for Using ChatGPT in Email Marketing

Craft Clear and Detailed Prompts

Provide specific instructions to guide ChatGPT in generating the desired content.
Example Prompt:
"Create a friendly and professional thank-you email for a client who just made a purchase. Include a 10% discount code for their next order and mention the product they purchased."

Maintain the Human Touch

Ensure emails mimic natural human conversation to connect effectively with recipients.
Tips:

- Relatable Language: Use everyday language that feels authentic.
- Personal Anecdotes: When appropriate, include stories or experiences.

Optimize for Engagement

Use recipients' first names and relevant details to make emails more engaging.
Strategies:

- Segmentation: Tailor content to specific audience segments.
- Behavioral Triggers: Customize emails based on user interactions.

Ensure Clarity and Brevity

Keep your emails concise, avoiding unnecessary jargon.
Example:
Break complex information into bullet points for easy readability.

Incorporate Visual Elements

Enhance emails with images, icons, and formatting to improve visual appeal.
Tip:
Ask ChatGPT to suggest where visual elements can enhance the message.

Ethical Considerations in AI-Driven Email Marketing

User Privacy and Data Protection

- Compliance with Regulations: Adhere to laws like GDPR and the CAN-SPAM Act.
- Data Security: Protect personal information and use data responsibly.

Respecting Recipient Preferences

- Opt-Out Options: Always include a clear unsubscribe link.
- Frequency Management: Avoid overwhelming recipients with too many emails.

Transparency and Honesty

- Clear Identification: Ensure recipients know who the email is from.
- Honest Content: Avoid misleading subject lines or deceptive content.

Monitoring AI Outputs

- Quality Assurance: Regularly review AI-generated emails for accuracy and appropriateness.
- Bias Mitigation: Be vigilant about unintended biases in language or messaging.

Real-World Applications and Case Studies

Case Study 1: Boosting Open Rates with Personalized Subject Lines
Challenge: A retail company faced low open rates for promotional campaigns.
Solution: Utilized ChatGPT to generate personalized subject lines tailored to different customer segments.

Result: After A/B testing, they implemented the top-performing subject lines and achieved a 40% increase in open rates.

Case Study 2: Streamlining Thank-You Emails in E-commerce
Challenge: An e-commerce business found sending personalized thank-you emails time-consuming.
Solution: Implemented ChatGPT to automate thank-you emails, incorporating customer names and purchase details.
Result: Saved 10 hours per week and improved customer satisfaction scores by 15%.

Integrating ChatGPT into Your Workflow

Setting Up Templates

Create standardized email templates for different purposes that ChatGPT can customize.
Example:

- Welcome Emails: Develop a base template welcoming new subscribers.
- Promotional Emails: Template highlighting offers with placeholders for personalization.

Automating Content Generation

Use ChatGPT to draft initial email versions, then review and refine them.
Benefits:

- Efficiency: Speeds up the content creation process.
- Consistency: Maintains a uniform brand voice across communications.

Collaborating with Your Team

Integrate ChatGPT outputs into your team's workflow for feedback and improvement.
Strategies:

- Collaboration Tools: Use platforms like Slack or Trello to share drafts.
- Team Reviews: Establish a review process for quality assurance.

Monitoring and Optimization

Continuously monitor email performance and adjust strategies accordingly.
Implementation:

- Performance Metrics: Track open rates, click-through rates, and conversions.

- Data-Driven Adjustments: Use insights to refine content and targeting.

Conclusion

Harnessing AI for Enhanced Email Marketing

Integrating ChatGPT into your email marketing strategy can significantly enhance efficiency, personalization, and overall performance. By leveraging its capabilities, you transform your email campaigns into more effective and less time-consuming efforts that resonate with your audience and drive meaningful results.

Key Takeaways

- Automation Enhances Efficiency: Save time by automating email creation without sacrificing quality.
- Personalization Drives Engagement: Tailored content increases relevance and connection.
- Versatility Supports Various Needs: Utilize ChatGPT for different email types to meet diverse business objectives.
- Ethical Practices Build Trust: Adhere to regulations and respect user privacy to maintain credibility.
- Continuous Optimization Improves Results: Refine your strategies using A/B testing and data insights.

Action Steps

1. Implement ChatGPT:
    - Start integrating ChatGPT into your email marketing workflow for a specific email type, such as thank-you emails.
2. Experiment with Prompts:
    - Craft detailed prompts to guide ChatGPT in generating tailored content.
3. Analyze Results:
    - Monitor the performance of AI-generated emails and refine your approach based on data insights.

4. Expand Usage:

    ◦ Gradually incorporate ChatGPT into other email types and campaigns to enhance your overall strategy.

5. Ensure Ethical Compliance:

    ◦ Stay informed about regulations and implement practices that protect user privacy and data.

Final Thoughts

Harnessing the power of AI in your email marketing is a transformative step toward more tremendous business success. With ChatGPT as your ally, you can create compelling, personalized, and effective email campaigns that stand out in the crowded digital landscape. Embrace this technology, experiment with its capabilities, and watch your email marketing reach new heights.

Your journey to mastering AI-driven email campaigns starts now. Take proactive steps, implement these strategies, and unlock the full potential of your marketing efforts. The future of email marketing is here—make it work for you.

Chapter 16: Strategy 14 – AI-Powered Affiliate Marketing

Unlocking the Power of ChatGPT for Affiliate Marketing Success

Affiliate marketing is a dynamic and competitive field where content quality, relevance, and timing are crucial for success. Leveraging AI technologies like ChatGPT can revolutionize affiliate marketing strategies by automating content creation, enhancing personalization, and optimizing performance. This chapter explores how you can harness ChatGPT to transform your affiliate marketing efforts, boost income streams, and establish authority in your niche.

Why Choose ChatGPT for Affiliate Marketing?

Efficiency and Cost-Effectiveness

- Automated Content Creation: ChatGPT can quickly generate large volumes of high-quality content, reducing the time and resources spent on writing.

- Consistent Brand Voice: By training ChatGPT on your existing content, you ensure all outputs align with your brand's tone and style.

Scalability

- Expand Content Production: Easily scale up your content library to meet growing business demands without the need for additional staff.

- Diversify Income Streams: Utilize ChatGPT to explore and develop multiple affiliate marketing channels simultaneously.

Enhanced Creativity and SEO Optimization

- Innovative Ideas: Generate fresh content to keep your audience engaged and ahead of industry trends.

- SEO-Friendly Content: Create optimized content that improves search engine rankings and drives organic traffic.

Understanding How ChatGPT Enhances Affiliate Marketing

Technical Insights

ChatGPT uses advanced Natural Language Processing (NLP) and machine learning algorithms to understand context, generate human-like text, and analyze data. In affiliate marketing, ChatGPT can:

- Keyword Optimization: Identify high-performing keywords and phrases relevant to your niche.

- Content Personalization: Tailor messages to specific audience segments based on behavior and preferences.

- Trend Analysis: Analyze market trends and consumer sentiments to inform your marketing strategies.

- Automated Responses: Provide instant customer support through AI-powered chatbots.

Limitations and Considerations:

- Knowledge Cutoff: ChatGPT's training data extends up to 2021. Verify time-sensitive information with current data sources.

- Content Review: Always proofread AI-generated content to ensure accuracy, originality, and compliance with your brand guidelines.

- Ethical Use: Be mindful of moral considerations, such as avoiding plagiarism and maintaining transparency with your audience.

Developing Topical Authority with ChatGPT

Establishing authority in your niche is essential for building trust and driving conversions. ChatGPT streamlines the process of identifying relevant topics and creating in-depth content.

Steps to Develop Topical Authority

1. Identify Trending Topics

- Prompt Example:"List the top 10 emerging trends in eco-friendly jewelry for 2024."
- Output: ChatGPT lists current and relevant topics, such as sustainable materials, ethical sourcing, and minimalist designs.

2. Create Subtopics and Content Clusters
    - Prompt Example:"For the topic 'Sustainable Jewelry Materials,' provide five subtopics to explore."
    - Output: Detailed subtopics like recycled metals, lab-grown diamonds, and biodegradable packaging.
3. Optimize with Keywords
    - Prompt Example:"Identify high-performing keywords for 'lab-grown diamonds benefits.'"
    - Output: A list of keywords with search volumes and competition levels to enhance SEO.

Benefits:

- Time Savings: Quickly generate comprehensive topic lists without extensive manual research.
- Relevance: Align your content with the latest industry trends and audience interests.
- SEO Enhancement: Optimize content to improve visibility and attract targeted traffic.

Leveraging ChatGPT for Affiliate Marketing Strategies

1. Social Media Management
    - Generate Engaging Posts: Create consistent and captivating content across platforms like Instagram, Facebook, and Twitter.
        - Prompt Example:"Draft 5 Instagram captions promoting our new eco-friendly bracelets, including relevant hashtags."

- Maintain Brand Presence: Ensure regular updates to keep your audience engaged.

2. SEO Optimization
   - Meta Titles and Descriptions: Craft SEO-friendly metadata for web pages and blog posts.
     - Prompt Example:"Generate a compelling meta description for a blog post titled 'The Rise of Sustainable Fashion Jewelry.'"
   - Content Audits: Receive recommendations to improve SEO performance.

3. Content Curation and Creation
   - Curate Relevant Content: Share industry news and articles that resonate with your audience.
     - Prompt Example:"Summarize the key points from the latest report on ethical jewelry sourcing."
   - Generate Original Content: Produce blog posts, articles, and product reviews.

4. Personalized Affiliate Campaigns
   - Tailored Messaging: Customize content for different audience segments to increase relevance.
     - Prompt Example:"Write an email promoting our affiliate program to fashion bloggers, highlighting the benefits for their audience."
   - Compelling CTAs: Develop persuasive calls-to-action to drive conversions.

5. Product Descriptions for Online Stores
   - Highlight Unique Features: Create detailed and enticing descriptions that emphasize product benefits.
     - Prompt Example:"Write a product description for a handmade necklace made from recycled ocean plastics."
   - Consistent Branding: Ensure all product listings reflect your brand identity.

6. Email Marketing Automation
   - Personalized Campaigns: Generate targeted emails for different stages of the cus-

tomer journey.

  - Prompt Example:"Draft a follow-up email for customers who abandoned their cart, offering a discount incentive."

- Improved Engagement: Increase open and click-through rates with compelling subject lines and content.

7. AI Chatbots for Customer Support
   - 24/7 Assistance: Implement chatbots to answer customer inquiries in real time.
     - Prompt Example:"Create a chatbot script to help customers choose the right ring size."
   - Enhanced User Experience: Improve customer satisfaction and drive sales.

Ethical Considerations in AI-Powered Affiliate Marketing

Ensuring Content Originality

- Avoid Plagiarism: Use plagiarism detection tools to ensure all AI-generated content is unique.
- Regular Review: Review and edit content to maintain authenticity and uphold your brand's standards.

Transparency with Audiences

- Disclosure: Be transparent about using affiliate links and AI-generated content where appropriate.
- Trust Building: Maintain honesty in product reviews and recommendations to foster trust with your audience.

Data Privacy and Compliance

- User Consent: Ensure compliance with data protection regulations like GDPR when collecting and using customer data.
- Secure Handling: Protect sensitive information used in personalization and targeting.

Responsible AI Usage

- Bias Mitigation: Monitor AI outputs for unintended biases and rectify them to promote inclusivity.
- Ethical Marketing Practices: Avoid manipulative tactics that could harm your brand reputation.

Steps to Maximize Affiliate Marketing Revenue with ChatGPT

1. Stay Updated with Industry Trends
    - Prompt Example:"What are the top consumer preferences in sustainable jewelry for the upcoming season?"
    - Application: Tailor your offerings and content to match current trends.

2. Refine Your Niche
    - Market Analysis: Use ChatGPT to evaluate the profitability of sub-niches.
        - Prompt Example:"Analyze the market potential for customizable jewelry options."

3. Optimize Content for SEO
    - Keyword Research: Identify high-value keywords to target.
        - Prompt Example:"List long-tail keywords related to 'ethical diamond alterna tives.'"

4. Scale Content Production
    - Automate Creation: Use ChatGPT to generate a high volume of quality content.
        - Prompt Example:"Produce an outline for an e-book on sustainable fashion accessories."

5. Enhance Audience Engagement
    - Interactive Content: Create quizzes, polls, or interactive posts.
        - Prompt Example:"Develop a quiz to help customers find their ideal jewelry style."

6. Implement A/B Testing
   - Optimize Performance: Test different content variations to see what resonates best.
     - Prompt Example:"Generate two versions of a headline for a blog post on 'Top 10 Eco-Friendly Jewelry Brands.'"

7. Leverage Cross-Selling Opportunities
   - Related Products: Suggest complementary items to increase the average order value.
     - Prompt Example:"Write a product recommendation for customers who purchased our silver earrings."

8. Provide Exceptional Customer Support
   - Personalized Assistance: Use AI chatbots to offer tailored support.
     - Prompt Example:"Create chatbot responses for common questions about our return policy."

Real-World Success Stories

Case Study 1: Tripling Revenue with AI-Assisted Content
Challenge: A boutique jewelry store needed more content to engage its growing online audience.
Solution: Integrated ChatGPT to automate the creation of blog posts, social media content, and email newsletters.
Result: Within six months, they tripled their revenue by increasing website traffic, improving SEO rankings, and boosting affiliate sales.

Case Study 2: Streamlining Affiliate Campaigns for an E-commerce Store
Challenge: Managing multiple affiliate marketing campaigns manually took time and effort.
Solution: Utilized ChatGPT to automate content generation, perform keyword optimization, and personalize email marketing.
Result: Achieved a 150% increase in affiliate sales and reduced content creation time by 70%, allowing the team to focus on strategic growth initiatives.

Integrating ChatGPT into Your Workflow

Setting Up a Consistent Formatting Style

- Standardize Templates: Create templates for different types of content to ensure consistency.

- Example: Develop a blog post template with sections for introduction, body, and conclusion, including SEO considerations.

Collaborating with Your Team

- Shared Platforms: Use collaboration tools to integrate ChatGPT outputs into your team's workflow.

- Review Process: Establish content review and approval guidelines to maintain quality control.

Monitoring and Optimization

- Performance Tracking: Use analytics to monitor the effectiveness of AI-generated content.

- Continuous Improvement: Adjust strategies based on data insights to enhance results.

Visualizing Your Affiliate Marketing Strategy
(Insert Diagram: Affiliate Marketing Workflow with ChatGPT Integration)

- Content Creation: AI-generated blogs, social media posts, and product descriptions.

- SEO Optimization: Keyword research, meta tags, content audits.

- Audience Engagement: Personalized emails, chatbots, interactive content.

- Performance Analysis: Data tracking, A/B testing, trend analysis.

Conclusion: Transforming Affiliate Marketing with AI

Embracing AI-powered tools like ChatGPT in your affiliate marketing strategy is a transformative step that can significantly accelerate your business growth. You can focus on strategic initiatives and build a sustainable competitive advantage by automating content creation, enhancing personalization, and optimizing performance.

Key Takeaways

- Leverage Efficiency: Automate repetitive tasks to save time and resources.
- Enhance Personalization: Tailor content to individual audience segments for greater engagement.
- Scale Strategically: Expand your marketing efforts without compromising quality.
- Maintain Ethical Standards: Uphold transparency, originality, and responsible AI use.
- Continuously Optimize: Use data-driven insights to refine your strategies.

Action Steps

1. Integrate ChatGPT: Begin by incorporating ChatGPT into one aspect of your affiliate marketing, such as content creation.
2. Experiment and Refine: Test different strategies and adjust based on performance metrics.
3. Expand Usage: Gradually implement ChatGPT across various marketing channels.
4. Monitor Ethics and Compliance: Ensure all AI-generated content meets ethical guidelines and regulatory requirements.
5. Stay Informed: Keep up with AI advancements to leverage new features and maintain a competitive edge.

Your Journey Ahead

Integrating AI in affiliate marketing is more than an enhancement—a revolution offering endless possibilities. By embracing ChatGPT, you're positioning your business at the forefront of digital marketing innovation, ready to outperform competitors and exceed customer expectations.

Stay Committed and Curious

Success requires dedication and adaptability. To fully realize the potential of AI-powered affiliate marketing, continue learning, experimenting, and refining your approach.

Additional Resources

- AI Tools for Marketers:
  - Semrush for keyword research
  - Grammarly for content refinement

  - Copyscape for plagiarism detection
- Learning Platforms:
  - Coursera's "AI for Digital Marketing"
  - Udemy's "Affiliate Marketing Masterclass"
- Ethical Guidelines:
  - OpenAI's Usage Policies
  - FTC Guidelines on Affiliate Marketing Disclosures
- Community Forums:
  - r/AffiliateMarketing on Reddit
  - Digital Marketing groups on LinkedIn

By thoughtfully integrating ChatGPT into your affiliate marketing strategy and adhering to ethical practices, you're not just adopting a new tool but transforming how you approach marketing and business growth. Embrace the possibilities, stay informed, and continuously refine your strategies to achieve exceptional results.

Chapter 17: Strategy 15 - ChatGPT for Personal Branding

Elevate Your Brand with ChatGPT

In today's digital landscape, personal branding is more crucial than ever. Establishing a solid personal brand can set you apart whether you're an entrepreneur, influencer, or professional. ChatGPT is a powerful tool that can help you build and enhance your brand by streamlining various aspects of your branding strategy.

1. Name Generation

Crafting the Perfect Brand Name

Picture this: you're on the verge of launching your brand-new business into the digital universe. But before you hit the launch button, there's one crucial step to nail down: your brand name. Think of it as your digital calling card—the first impression you make on potential customers. Your name isn't just a label; it embodies your brand's identity, its essence distilled into a few carefully chosen words.

Why a Great Brand Name Matters:

- First Impressions: Your brand name is often customers' first interaction with your business.
- Brand Identity reflects your brand's values, mission, and personality.
- Memorability: A catchy name is more accessible for customers to remember and share.

How ChatGPT Can Help:

- Brainstorming Ideas: Generate a diverse list of potential brand names based on your industry, values, and target audience.
- Refining Options: Narrow down the list by evaluating each name's uniqueness,

relevance, and availability.

- Iterative Process: Continue refining and generating new names until you find the perfect fit.

Example Prompt:
"Generate 20 unique and catchy brand names for an online boutique specializing in handmade jewelry."

Action Step:
1. Input Detailed Criteria: Provide ChatGPT with specific guidelines such as industry, target audience, desired tone (e.g., elegant, modern), and any keywords you want to include.

2. Review and Select: Evaluate the generated names for uniqueness, relevance, and availability. Consider consulting with an industry expert for feedback.

3. Finalize Your Choice: Choose a name that best represents your brand's identity and resonates with your target audience.

2. Brand Personality

Defining and Enhancing Your Brand's Personality
Ah, brand personality—the secret sauce that sets you apart from the digital crowd. With ChatGPT in your corner, you can dial up your brand's personality to eleven, quickly covering every facet of your brand strategy. From the tone and style of your content to the very essence of your brand voice, ChatGPT can help you tailor your message to resonate with your target audience.

Key Elements of Brand Personality:
- The tone of Voice: The way your brand communicates (e.g., friendly, professional, quirky).

- Style: Visual and verbal elements that convey your brand's character.

- Consistency: Maintaining the same personality across all platforms and content.

How ChatGPT Can Help:
- Crafting Tone and Style: Define the tone and style that best reflects your brand's personality.

- Content Consistency: Ensure all your content aligns with your defined brand personality.

- Enhanced Messaging: Tailor your messaging to better connect with your audience.

Example Prompt:
"Help me define a friendly and approachable brand personality for my handmade jewelry business."

Action Step:
1. Define Your Brand Attributes: List the key characteristics you want your brand to embody.

2. Use ChatGPT to Develop Guidelines: Use ChatGPT to create a brand style guide that outlines tone, language, and visual elements.

3. Implement Across Channels: Apply the defined personality consistently across your website, social media, and marketing materials.

3. Customer Persona

Understanding and Targeting Your Ideal Customer
In the wild and woolly world of brand strategy, one essential component can't be overlooked: the customer persona. Think of it as your brand's compass, guiding you through the murky waters of the digital landscape. With ChatGPT by your side, you can dive deep into the minds of your target audience, crafting customized command prompts to unlock invaluable insights into their wants, needs, and desires.

Importance of Customer Personas:
- Targeted Marketing: Tailor your marketing efforts to address specific customer needs.

- Product Development: Create products that align with your audience's preferences.

- Enhanced Engagement: Communicate more effectively by understanding your audience's language and pain points.

How ChatGPT Can Help:
- Research and Insights: Generate detailed customer personas based on demographic and psychographic data.

- Content Personalization: Create content that speaks directly to your target audience's interests and challenges.
- Strategic Planning: Use personas to inform your brand strategy and marketing campaigns.

Example Prompt:

"Create a detailed customer persona for a 30-year-old professional woman interested in sustainable and handmade jewelry."

Action Step:

1. Gather Data: Collect information about your current customers, including demographics, interests, and behaviors.
2. Generate Personas: Use ChatGPT to create comprehensive customer personas based on this data.
3. Apply Insights: Integrate these personas into your marketing strategies, content creation, and product development processes.

4. On-Page SEO

Optimizing Your Website for Maximum Visibility

Before you unleash your website upon the world, there's one last hurdle to clear: on-page SEO. The secret sauce ensures your site stands head and shoulders above the competition in the cutthroat world of e-commerce. With ChatGPT, you can optimize your content for maximum visibility with just a few keystrokes.

Critical Components of On-Page SEO:

- Keyword Optimization: Incorporate relevant keywords naturally into your content.
- Meta Tags: Craft compelling meta titles and descriptions to improve click-through rates.
- Content Quality: Ensure your content is informative, engaging, and valuable to your audience.
- Internal Linking: Connect related content within your website to enhance navigation and SEO.

How ChatGPT Can Help:

- Keyword Research: Identify high-value keywords relevant to your niche.
- Meta Description Creation: Generate SEO-friendly meta descriptions that attract clicks.
- Content Optimization: Refine your content to improve readability and SEO performance.
- SEO Audits: Perform comprehensive on-page SEO audits and receive actionable recommendations.

Example Prompt:
"Optimize this product description for SEO: 'Handcrafted silver bracelet with eco-friendly gemstones.' Include relevant keywords and a meta description."

Action Step:
1. Identify Keywords: Use ChatGPT to generate a list of targeted keywords for your content.
2. Optimize Content: Incorporate these keywords into your website content, ensuring it remains natural and engaging.
3. Create Meta Tags: Use ChatGPT to craft compelling meta titles and descriptions for each page.
4. Conduct SEO Audits: Regularly review your website's SEO performance and make necessary adjustments with ChatGPT's assistance.

5. Lead Generation and Email Marketing

Streamlining Lead Generation and Crafting Effective Email Campaigns
Now that your website is primed for success, it's time to turn your attention to lead generation and email marketing. Sure, it might sound daunting, but with ChatGPT in your corner, you'll be a digital dynamo in no time.

Importance of Lead Generation and Email Marketing:
- Lead Generation: Attract and capture potential customers for your business.
- Email Marketing: Nurture leads and convert them into loyal customers through targeted email campaigns.

How ChatGPT Can Help:

- Lead Magnet Creation: Develop compelling lead magnets (e.g., eBooks, checklists) to attract potential customers.
- Email Copywriting: Craft persuasive email copy that engages and converts subscribers.
- Automated Campaigns: Set up automated email sequences to nurture leads without constant manual effort.
- Personalization: Tailor your emails to individual subscriber preferences and behaviors for higher engagement.

Example Prompt:

"Create a lead magnet idea for a handmade jewelry business and draft an email sequence to nurture new leads."

Action Step:

1. Create Lead Magnets: Use ChatGPT to brainstorm and develop valuable lead magnets that attract your target audience.
2. Design Email Sequences: Craft automated emails that nurture leads from initial contact to conversion.
3. Personalize Content: Tailor your email content based on subscriber data to enhance relevance and engagement.
4. Analyze and Optimize: Monitor the performance of your email campaigns and use ChatGPT to refine and improve your strategies.

6. Leveraging Chatbots for Customer Service

Enhancing Customer Interaction with AI-Powered Chatbots

Ah, the humble chatbot—a digital darling revolutionizing how businesses interact with customers. And with ChatGPT leading the charge, you can take your customer service to the next level in no time flat.

Benefits of AI-Powered Chatbots:

- 24/7 Availability: Provide round-the-clock customer support without the need for human intervention.

- Instant Responses: Address customer inquiries and issues in real time, enhancing user experience.

- Cost Efficiency: Reduce the need for large customer service teams, saving time and resources.

How ChatGPT Can Help:

- Automate Conversations: Handle common customer queries and provide solutions efficiently.

- Personalized Assistance: Tailor responses based on customer data and previous interactions.

- Expand Functionality: Use chatbots for various functions beyond customer service, such as recruitment and onboarding.

Example Prompt:

"Create a conversational script for a chatbot that assists customers in selecting the perfect necklace based on their preferences."

Action Step:

1. Define Chatbot Roles: Determine the specific tasks and functions your chatbot will handle (e.g., answering FAQs guiding purchases).

2. Develop Scripts: Use ChatGPT to create engaging and helpful conversational scripts tailored to your brand's voice.

3. Implement and Test: Integrate the chatbot into your website and conduct testing to ensure it operates smoothly.

4. Monitor and Improve: Continuously review chatbot interactions and use ChatGPT to refine and enhance its responses based on customer feedback.

7. Building a Loyal Audience and Monetizing Your Brand

Cultivating Loyalty and Unlocking Revenue Streams

Now that you've laid the groundwork for success, it's time to reap the rewards. With ChatGPT by your side, the sky's the limit when building a loyal audience and monetizing your brand.

Critical Strategies for Building Loyalty and Monetization:

- Personalized Experiences: Tailor interactions and content to individual customer preferences.
- Exclusive Content: Offer valuable resources and content to your most dedicated followers.
- Diverse Revenue Streams: Explore multiple income-generating avenues, such as affiliate marketing, sponsored content, and paid memberships.

How ChatGPT Can Help:

- Personalization: Create personalized shopping experiences and provide top-notch customer support.
- Content Creation: Develop high-value content that engages your audience and encourages loyalty.
- Monetization Strategies: Identify and implement effective monetization methods tailored to your brand and audience.

Example Prompt:

"Suggest five ways to monetize a handmade jewelry blog, including affiliate marketing and sponsored content opportunities."

Action Step:

1. Engage Your Audience: Use ChatGPT to create engaging, personalized content that resonates with your audience.
2. Develop Monetization Plans: Explore various monetization strategies and use ChatGPT to plan and implement them effectively.
3. Offer Exclusive Content: Create premium content or services for loyal followers using ChatGPT to maintain high quality and relevance.
4. Analyze and Adjust: Monitor the performance of your monetization efforts and use ChatGPT to refine your strategies based on data insights.

8. Top-Tier Methods to Monetize Your Brand

Unlocking Multiple Revenue Streams with ChatGPT

Let's look at top-tier methods to monetize your brand, each enhanced by the capabilities of ChatGPT:

Affiliate Marketing

Picture this: you're scrolling through your favorite social media platform when suddenly, you stumble upon a product that catches your eye. But here's the kicker: it's not just any product—it's one you can promote and earn a commission on through affiliate marketing. With ChatGPT by your side, the whole process becomes a breeze.

Benefits:

- Passive Income: Earn commissions on sales generated through your affiliate links.
- Flexibility: Promote a wide range of products that align with your brand.

How ChatGPT Can Help:

- Affiliate Opportunities: Identify and evaluate potential affiliate programs that suit your niche.
- Content Creation: Craft persuasive content that seamlessly integrates affiliate links.
- Campaign Management: Develop and manage effective affiliate marketing campaigns with ease.

Example Prompt:

"Create a blog post promoting eco-friendly jewelry brands with affiliate links included."

Sponsored Content

Seamless Integration of Sponsored Products

You've seen it a thousand times on YouTube videos and blog posts—content creators seamlessly integrating sponsored products or services into their content. With ChatGPT, you can join their ranks and start earning money from sponsored content.

Benefits:

- Revenue Generation: Earn money by partnering with brands that align with your values.
- Content Enhancement: Create high-quality content that adds value to your audience while promoting sponsors.

How ChatGPT Can Help:

- Content Planning: Develop ideas for sponsored content that resonate with your audience.

- Script Writing: Craft compelling scripts or blog posts that effectively incorporate sponsored messages.
- Campaign Strategy: Plan and execute sponsored content campaigns that maximize engagement and revenue.

Example Prompt:

"Write a YouTube video script reviewing three eco-friendly jewelry brands, including mentions of each sponsor."

Paid Memberships

Creating Exclusive Value for Your Audience

But why stop there? With ChatGPT, you can take your monetization efforts to the next level with paid memberships. By offering exclusive content and resources to your most dedicated fans, you can create a steady stream of recurring revenue for your brand.

Benefits:

- Recurring Revenue: Generate consistent income through membership fees.
- Enhanced Loyalty: Foster a deeper connection with your most engaged audience members.

How ChatGPT Can Help:

- Exclusive Content Creation: Develop high-quality content tailored specifically for members.
- Marketing Campaigns: Craft persuasive marketing materials to promote your membership program.
- Community Building: Create engaging content that encourages interaction and community among members.

Example Prompt:

"Design a welcome email sequence for new members of our exclusive jewelry design community, including a special discount offer."

Final Impact: Transform Your Brand with AI

As we conclude Strategy 15 - ChatGPT for Personal Branding, it's evident that integrating ChatGPT into your personal branding strategy is not just a beneficial move—it's a transformative one. The ability to automate, personalize, and optimize various aspects of your brand-building efforts with precision and efficiency opens up endless possibilities for personal and professional growth.

Embrace the Future of Personal Branding

By leveraging ChatGPT, you're saving valuable time and resources and elevating the quality of your brand interactions. Imagine generating a compelling brand name, crafting a distinct brand personality, and developing detailed customer personas while optimizing your website for maximum visibility. This is the power of AI-driven personal branding.

Take Action Today

Don't let the complexities of personal branding hold you back. Start implementing the strategies you've learned:

1. Integrate ChatGPT: Begin using ChatGPT for one aspect of your branding, such as name generation or content creation.

2. Experiment and Optimize: Use actionable tips and best practices to experiment with branding tactics. Based on the results, continuously refine your approach.

3. Scale Your Efforts: As you become more comfortable with ChatGPT, expand its use across all your branding activities. Watch as your brand's visibility and influence grow.

Unlock Your Branding Potential

Integrating AI in personal branding is more than just an enhancement—it's a revolution. By embracing ChatGPT, you're positioning yourself at the forefront of digital branding innovation. This sets you apart from competitors and ensures your brand is always ahead.

Your journey to mastering AI-powered personal branding starts now. Take the leap, implement these strategies, and unlock the full potential of your branding efforts. The future of personal branding is here—make it work for you.

About the Author

Augustus Blackmore was born in Phoenixville, Pennsylvania, in 1967. He developed an early interest in technology. He studied web development to better comprehend its complexities, intrigued by programming's stunning blend of art and logic. His insatiable curiosity eventually led him to artificial intelligence. He delves deep into it, revealing the vast potential of website programming and the development of AI models and algorithms.

A natural optimist, Augustus sees artificial intelligence as a magnificent instrument that may augment rather than replace human intelligence. In his debut book, "AI Millionaire Mindset: 20 Proven Strategies to Boost Profits and Efficiency," the author outlines his belief passionately. The author deciphers artificial intelligence in this crucial study and gives insights and strategies businesses may employ to maximize their potential and increase profitability. Augustus' poetry struck a chord in the hearts and minds of readers. Its practical applications and novel ideas have captivated the public, garnering this book with widespread acclaim.

Augustus is now writing on "The AI Survivalist Handbook: Secrets to Flourishing in an Era Dominated by Automation." This technical work aims to give its illustrious readers the knowledge and skills to adapt and succeed in an increasingly computerized society. In an age when artificial intelligence has caused dread, Augustus is a beacon of hope. His belief reveals the wide range of alternatives this breakthrough technology provides humanity. He is adamant that a society with knowledge and vision can survive and thrive in the face of artificial intelligence. Through his writing, he seeks to achieve this purpose.

We'd love to hear your genuine opinions on this book, whether you enjoyed it or not. Your feedback is valuable to us.

Thank you!

Join my mailing list and receive a free eBook:
Beginner's Guide to AI Investing: A simplified guide for those looking to invest in AI technologies or companies.
Visit my website: www.synapticstories.com

Your support as a reader is invaluable, especially as a small indie publisher. Knowing that my book may providing enjoyment in your life is incredibly fulfilling.

If you could spare a minute to leave your honest feedback on Amazon, it would be immensely helpful.

Your review not only aids in improving my future work but also guides other parents in their choice of educational resources.

Once again, thank you for being a part of this journey.
Your thoughts and experiences with the book are truly appreciated!

To leave feedback

1. Open up your camera app.
2. Point your mobile device at the QR code below.
3. The review page will appear in your web browser.

Or visit Amazon search by
Ai Millionaire Mindset and Augustus Blackmore to the Amazon search

Made in the USA
Monee, IL
04 November 2026

67380150R00098